D1566325

The
James Francis Tulloch Diary
1875-1910

James Francis Tulloch and Annie Brown Tulloch. James and Annie were married shortly after he came to Orcas Island in 1875.

The
James Francis Tulloch Diary
1875-1910

The true story of the ups and downs of James and Annie Tulloch and their nine children, all of whom were born and raised on Orcas Island in Washington State's San Juan Islands.

Compiled and Edited

by

Gordon Keith

Binford & Mort
Thomas Binford, Publisher

2536 S.E. Eleventh • Portland, Oregon 97202

Dedicated to:
Isabel Tulloch for whom this diary was written.

The James Francis Tulloch Diary
1875-1910

Copyright under International
Pan-American Copyright Conventions
Copyright © 1978 by Gordon Keith

Library of Congress Catalog Card Number: 78-56345
ISBN: 0-8323-0302-X (hardcover)
ISBN: 0-8323-0303-8 (softcover)

Printed in the United States of America

First Edition 1978

INTRODUCTION

My introduction to Orcas Island, located in the upper Northwest corner of Washington State, came in 1963 following a short vacation that my wife, Barbara, and I spent in British Columbia. At the time, we were on our way back to California aboard a Washington State ferry via the San Juan Islands. We decided to stop off on Orcas Island for a better look at this island paradise.

So intrigued were we with this island that, before we departed the following day, we had put earnest money down on a small farmhouse overlooking the Bay, near the Village of Olga.

Our plan was to return to our home in San Jose, California, sell our business and property, then return to Orcas Island to live permanently where I could follow my free-lance writing career. However, because of a bad business deal in closing out our California holdings, we were unable to move to our island home until seven years later.

It is interesting to note that when friends of ours learned that we were returning to the "wilds" of the San Juans to live on this 57-square-mile island, with a population of less than 1200 people, they thought I had taken leave of my senses. Knowing that I am not a writer of fiction, our friends reasoned that I would run out of subjects to write about before the year was over.

As I look back over the past ten years, the problem was never one of what I would write about, rather, would I live long enough to write of the endless happenings of those who have lived or still live on this San Juan Archipelago. One such "happening" is *The James Francis Tulloch Diary.*

The diary covers Tulloch's encounters with such diverse and sundry characters as the self-proclaimed "Colonel" May, whose questionable ventures included rum-running and smuggling, as well as the promotion of Indian maidens to prospective white husbands—the fee for which depended upon the youth and pulchritude of the prospective bride.

Touched with humor is Tulloch's meeting with Captain Forney of the U.S. Geodetic and Coast Survey, who arrived near his property on Orcas Island aboard a 300-ton vessel to "triangulate the Straits." Hired by Captain Forney to lead him and his crew to the top of Mt. Constitution (2409 feet), Tulloch became lost enroute. He had neglected to inform the captain that he had never even been to the top of Mt. Constitution.

James Tulloch writes warmly of his meeting with Charles Bancroft Walker—a cousin of the famed historian, George Bancroft—who moved to Orcas Island after purchasing five acres at the foot of Mt. Constitution from the Tulloch family. The two men became the best of friends and remained so until Charles Bancroft Walker's untimely death a few years later. In the pages that follow, you will meet many other of Tulloch's interesting islanders.

This is how I chanced upon the diary: I had been doing some free-lance reporting and feature articles for *The Islands' Sounder*, a local paper, when Bob Fowler, former San Juan County Building Inspector—whose folks came to Orcas Island in 1886—told me about a 100-year-old Orcas Island diary he had run across and offered to introduce me to the folks who had it.

Having long been interested in the history of the San Juan Islands and those who inhabit them, I was delighted to meet Stuart, the last of the original nine Tulloch children, all of whom were born on Orcas Island. The result of that meeting with Stuart and his wife, Jessie, is the subject of this book.

Gordon Keith
Orcas Island, Washington

ACKNOWLEDGMENTS

Portions of *The James Francis Tulloch Diary* have appeared serially in *The Islands' Sounder* newspaper.

The editor gratefully acknowledges permission from Dale and Catherine Pederson (owners of Darvill's Rare Print and Book Shop of Orcas Island, Washington) to reprint "Ye Old Map."

Special thanks go to Kathryn Tulloch White, who transcribed the original handwritten Diary into typewritten pages; and to Evelyn Myers, Ellen Siegwarth, and Roger and Hulda Purdue for permission to reprint pictures from their early-day Orcas Island collections.

It is with regret that a number of photographs in this book are without credit lines because the photographer of a particular photograph could not be identified.

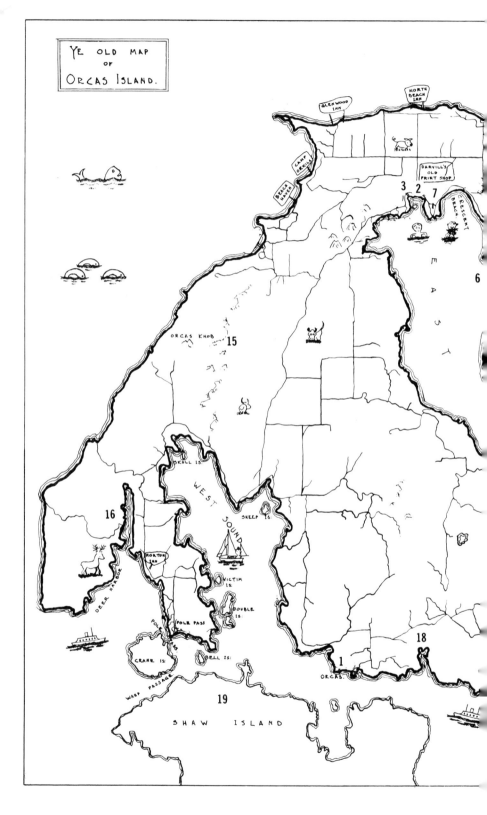

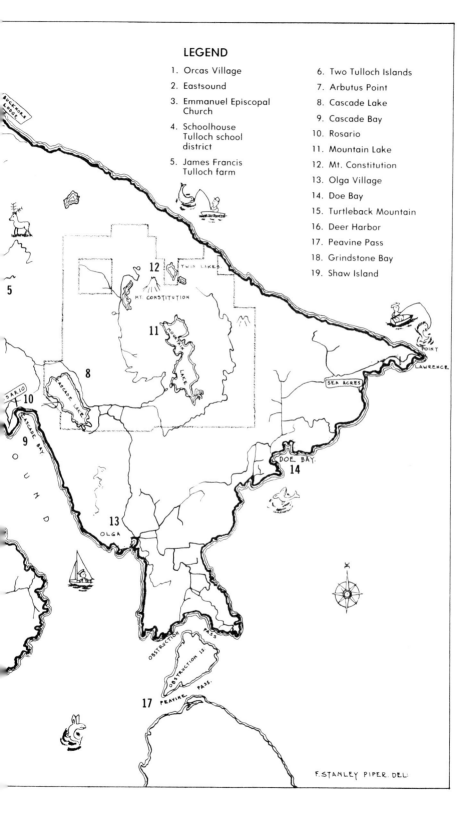

LEGEND

1. Orcas Village
2. Eastsound
3. Emmanuel Episcopal Church
4. Schoolhouse Tulloch school district
5. James Francis Tulloch farm
6. Two Tulloch Islands
7. Arbutus Point
8. Cascade Lake
9. Cascade Bay
10. Rosario
11. Mountain Lake
12. Mt. Constitution
13. Olga Village
14. Doe Bay
15. Turtleback Mountain
16. Deer Harbor
17. Peavine Pass
18. Grindstone Bay
19. Shaw Island

F. STANLEY PIPER. DEL.

1.

My youngest daughter, Isabel, using the well-known right of the "baby" of the family, has bulldozed me into writing down some of the things I have done and seen in my three score and ten years. I am the more willing to comply as it will help pass away the dull days and long evenings of the coming winter.

My span of life has witnessed the greatest material advancement the world has ever known or seen in that length of time. Though probably it will be far excelled during her life. Still, an age that has transformed the tallow dip into the electric light, the sickle into the reaper and mower, the monthly or even semi-monthly mail into the wireless telegraph and telephone, the sluggish sailing vessel into the super dreadnaught and the deadly submarine and the ox team and sled into the automobile and the aeroplane and has transformed society from isolated individualism into a state verging on National Socialism, must surely give one something to write about.

If only I had the ability to do justice to it. But as this requires a far abler pen than mine I will content myself with noting a few of the changes I have seen take place in substituting the White man for the Indian, the Hereford for the Buffalo, and the building of the great cities where first I saw forests and plains. And if, in describing frontier life I must speak plainly of it as I found it, I sincerely hope that what I write for my daughter's amusement will never be allowed to hurt the feelings of anyone.

So much by way of introduction. In writing an account of one's life it is necessary to go back several generations before one was born. While environment may affect one's character to quite an extent, still, that is only one life. For we are the inherited results of thousands of lives in our long climb up to our present stage of existence. So it begins. . . .

My Father was a Methodist preacher and Mother early chose me to fill this place because of my studious habits. But she certainly made a bad choice as none of the family was less qualified for such a calling than I, although while still a small boy I had read the Bible through several times and now, in my 70th year, I can still repeat whole chapters from it. However, the result was an early disposition to criticize the Bible's inconsistencies.

Father was greatly worried when he found me reading "*Age of Reason*" by Thomas Paine. After punishing me he got Watson's "*Apology for the Bible*", the church's reply to the other, which I read carefully and certainly Paine has all the best of the argument. But I had little patience with theology that persisted in teaching as the inspired word of God that the earth was only six thousand years old; that Joshua made the sun stand still, that is made the earth quit revolving; that man was perfect but had deteriorated to his present state.

Now you must not think, Isabel, that I am writing of things in their regular order for I am writing of so many different things that I must go back and forth.

. . .When my Father came home one night and said that as soon as the crops were in and harvested he was going to Iowa (we were then living in London, Ontario, Canada) to visit the Wards, former neighbors of ours who had sent back glowing accounts of the richness of the soil of that state. I saw my chance and said that I was going with him. I had privately resolved that my face would ever be Westward till I looked out upon the Pacific.

In October Father and I took the train for Windsor and crossed the St. Clair at Detroit, meeting hordes of American citizens going to Canada on urgent business. I found out later that their urgency was connected with the draft the government had called. From Detroit we went to Milwaukee and then on to Mississippi where we crossed over the ice by stagecoach to McGreggers Landing in Iowa. The following morning we started across the state to Independence and from there by train to Waterloo where Father's neighbor, John Ward lived.

Until our folks sold out and followed us to Iowa the year following I always met Father there each Sunday. But as I proposed to be self-supporting I began at once to look for something to do. I got a job with a Mr. Munger, a butcher, also from Canada. . . . But I had my mind set on the West. . . .

I well remember my parting with Mother. She made me kneel down and with her arm about me she prayed to the God in whom she believed to protect and guard me from evil, not from death, but from sin. I can well remember her sad smile when I told her I would soon come back to her, which I firmly believed. But I never saw her again, and ten years later when I went back to Iowa I went with Hugh to see the graves of Mother and Charlie in a little cemetery on the banks of the Cedar River.

Mrs. Hammas *"Graves of a Household"* surely describes our family. Mother and Charlie lie by the Cedar in Iowa, Father lies on a mountain side in Colorado, Will fills a nameless grave in Nome, Alaska, where he was murdered for his money, Alec died in a cave in Hawaii and rests there, Hugh is in Oklahoma and will most certainly end his days there. I shall see the last setting of the sun here in the Evergreen State.

But what matters it where we live or where we die just so long as we in our blundering way try to do what seems to be our duty. For life always seems to me to be one days work in our upward climb. And that God has put within each of us a spark of Divinity whose duty it is to struggle upwards toward the light. And though we may often fall, our duty is to rise and struggle on again. Try to avoid the same pitfalls and always pray for Spiritual strength.

For I certainly believe in prayer. Not the prayer of so many church people "that God would set aside his unchangeable laws for their selfish benefit", but that strength would be given to us to do our duty though the Heavens fall.

Now I will not preach to you any more, Isabel, but I do believe that just as we end this day's work that we call this

3

"life", just so we will begin the next spiritually. So, it is enough for us to take one step at a time and leave the results with God who doeth all things well.

(*James Tullock tells about taking a boat to Portland, Oregon*):

As the companion with whom I had traveled across the continent was in a hurry to arrive on the Sound (Puget Sound) we arranged to take passage on the old "John L. Stevens" to Portland. As the first class fare was so high I persuaded my friend to join me in taking steerage passage. We would only be out a couple of days so we laid in a supply of good cigars and fruits and went aboard.

By proper use of the cigars I lived with the officers in their comfortable smoking room. And for a small sum to the cook I got just as good meals as those in first class cabins. We went down into the steerage once to see how it looked and that was enough. The place was worse than a pig sty.

A fellow passenger on board was a resident of Lopez Island in the then newly organized County of San Juan. He was certainly some advance man (for the Island). But he wasted little time on me because I had no idea of going into farming and because what little knowledge I had obtained of the San Juan Islands from my study of the Geneva Award enabled me to trip him up in some of his wild statements.

Before we arrived at Portland he had attached himself like a leech to my companion who had a family back in Iowa for whom he was to send as soon as he got located. He made the poor fellow believe that the Garden of Eden had nothing on Lopez Island. But as the man had to look around for employment at once he got me to promise that if I had the opportunity I would go see this marvelous island.

We stopped at Portland a few days and looked the village over, then crossed the river to Kalamath and took the train to Tacoma, the wonderful city of destiny of which we had heard so much about. We then took a boat for Seattle, a place of some 1500 inhabitants who were seemingly almost dependent on the

4

little sawmill run by Yesler and what little help they obtained from fishing and the ever present clams.

The change of climate or food brought me down with dysentery and I had quite a time of it. Upon recovery I looked into the opportunity of opening a book store but Humphrey and Young, the only ones in the business were practically starving and I could have bought them out for a song. Of all the dead broke areas I had been in this was certainly the worst at that time. Yet Humphrey and Young has now been changed to Lowman and Hanford and the starving little town is now a metropolis of the Northwest, and all in one generation. What will it be when another generation has passed?

Eldorado of the future for commerce with Asia will make this part of the country exceed the wildest dreams of those now living and Seattle has already begun her career for supremacy of the coast.

I walked onto a wooded road that led to a little nursery near what would be 20th and Yesler now and the road ended. But they told me there was a large lake beyond although there was no trail leading to it. I could have taken a homestead anywhere in at least half of what is now Seattle. But who could have foreseen the Queen City of the West among those rugged timbered hills?

The Broadway region was all wilderness and such corners as 2nd and Pike could have been obtained for a few hundred dollars. But everything was dead then and having heard much of Victoria I took off for that place and found a sleepy comfortable village where everything seemed always afternoon.

After rambling around Victoria until tired and seeing no opening for business I took the boat for Port Townsend intending to keep my promise and visit Lopez Island. But having arrived I found no one who knew anything about the islands, or how to get there. I had about made up my mind to return to Seattle and take a ship from there to Los Angeles, California as that place was being greatly boomed just then.

While waiting on the wharf for the arrival of my boat I overhead a group of men talking about the San Juan Islands. So

I inquired and found that they were waiting for the steamer *"Gussie Telfair"* from Portland bound for lime. They said I could get an Indian to put me across to Lopez Island from there, it being only a few miles.

So when the Telfair came in I took passage on her. These men then began to put me through the third degree. Where was I from? How long had I been in the Territory? What business did I follow? What was I going to Lopez Island for?

Finally one of them, a long, lean lantern-jawed Yankee whom I afterward found was named Gifford began telling me of the places that could be bought on Orcas Island near the lime works, among which was a farm of the M.L. Adams with a bearing fruit orchard of several hundred trees.

I asked him if that was the only place for sale near the lime works. He finally admitted that there was a little place near the lime kiln, but that it was absolutely worthless. This satisfied me that Gifford, for reasons of his own, did not want me to buy that place, but I resolved to look into it.

2.

The Captain being a stranger to these waters did not dare to navigate the San Juan Pass so he ran down past Blakely and came through Peavine Pass. We landed our boat against a big limestone boulder that had been blasted from the ledge above and carried lines for and aft to the shore. At this time the famous crime con case between Henry Ward Beecher and Theodore Tilton was dragging its weary length through the courts and disgusting all honest men. So it sounded quite pat when the line boss sang out "Look out there you'll beach her without tilting".

They ran a plank from rock to shore and I stepped onto Orcas Island on the 21st of June, 1875, little thinking that the greatest part of my life would be spent there.

They showed me a trail made by hanging planks along the face of the cliff in places and though it looked more fit for a goat than for men I followed it and came out at the camp. I asked the Chinese cook for dinner. John said "You catch um when the boys come." So I waited and while standing in the cook-house noting the various kinds of trees on the hillside, some old acquaintances, but some new to me, two girls came down the trail on the mountainside and went into a little house beyond. I noticed that they were both white, that one seemed eighteen or twenty years of age while the other looked younger. They did not resemble each other at all for the eldest had magnificent hair and a different cast of features entirely.

I wondered casually whether they were residents of the island or visitors like myself. How little I then thought that I was looking at the woman who would be my dear companion for life

7

and the Mother of my children. Though I have often regretted, from a financial point of view, my locating on that rugged old island, the meeting of your Mother there makes it the most fortunate occurrence of my life.

The season had been rainy up to that time but the next morning was bright and sunny. In fact, we had continual sunny weather until late that fall. After breakfast of John Chinaman's hash, which was very appetizing if you didn't watch its preparation, I started out to see this Adams place and also the one Gifford evidently did not want me to see.

Following a trail over the hill which led me though Salal brush and wet me thoroughly I came to a fine creek crossed by a foot log and just beyond it on a sloping tract overlooking the Bay I was surprised to see a frame dwelling. A log house was the regulation here and when I called to inquire the way, I was surprised to meet the young lady I had seen the day before.

I followed their instructions over a very bad trail and finally came to the Adams place which had a fine young bearing orchard. But Adams indignantly denied ever having offered it for sale. I then returned to the frame house and found the owner, Mr. Charles E. Setzer at home. He soon explained Mr. Gifford's reason for trying to deceive me as he had been trying to get the place to put up a stave mill and supply the lime company with barrels. But he wanted to get it for practically nothing as he knew Mr. Setzer was anxious to change to the place he afterwards moved to, near Douglas Channel. I spent a few hours with him looking over his claim.

The islands comprising the San Juan group had been claimed by both the United States and Great Britain. While both agreed on the 49th parallel as a boundary until it struck the sea at Point Roberts, they differed as to which channel the line should follow from there to the Strait of Juan de Fuca. The Americans claiming that it followed De Harro Straits while the British claimed that it should follow Rosario Channel, which would have thrown the San Juan group (of islands) all into British Columbia. In the meantime both countries kept troops posted on San Juan Island, the British near Roche Harbor and the

Americans near San Juan Town on the southern part of the island.

This made the islands practically a no-mans land for while there was such a conflict of authority it was the regular thing for those accused of a crime by one side to claim protection from the other. The natural result was that it became a gathering place for the lawless. This unpleasant state of affairs had been settled shortly after my arrival through the Geneva Award, by which the Emporer of Germany as chosen arbitrator had declared in favor of the De Harro Straits. It had been agreed that all claimants of land should have a reasonable time after the land was surveyed in which to correct their boundaries before any others were allowed to file claims and these rights for prior rights could be transferred.

This was the right that Mr. Setzer wished to sell with its improvements of the aforementioned frame house. Also about three acres in cultivation. I found the claim had a beautiful sheltered deep water harbor screened from the southerly winds by a high wooded point and protected from the north by two little islets that became one at low tide and with a narrow channel between them and the main island. While a lovely snow white shell beach extended along the harbor front to where a ledge of rock jutted out to deep water. At the SE corner of the harbor the stream which I had crossed that morning tumbled down into the sea with a fall of about a dozen feet or more. This accounted for Mr. Gifford's wish to get it.

I saw that it contained quite a body of good agricultural land that could in a homesteaded claim be enough by taking one forty to include the harbor and the other three to take in this valley. Although Mr. Setzer could not tell me how high up the spring was from which this stream came, I could hear it roaring away up on the mountainside. I recognized its future possibilities and Mr. Setzer and I soon came to terms. I paid $250 in gold or $320 in my money, as greenbacks were only worth 78 cents then.

We started in his little rowboat for Stockade Bay, now Olga, to have Judge Bowman who was a notary, make out the deed.

9

After Mr. Setzer had rowed a while I asked to spell him saying that I had never rowed, which was true, but I'd like to try. He gave me the oars with a smile and said, "Did I understand you to say you had never rowed before?" I told him that was correct. He said nothing more, but simply set me down as a liar. Although I had never rowed I understood the theory of it all right and avoided the blunder of beginners of either raising my oars too high or catching a crab but it has often been my fate to be regarded as a romancer when I'm stating facts.

This frame house, the first built on Orcas Island, had quite a history. The first locater on this claim I had purchased was a gambler from the Cariboo Mines named Enoch May, who, with another Irishman named M.L. Adams, a miner from the Cariboo, had made some money there. They had settled on these claims and finally quarreled over something and became lifelong enemies.

May got a carpenter from Victoria to come to the island to build him a house, taking most of it by hand from the cedars in the swamp at the foot of the mountain and riving and planing it down, surely a tedious process. When the carpenter presented the very reasonable bill of $500 May refused to pay him. The man, a Mr. Kelly, after whom the creek on Orcas Island is named, brought suit before the British Captain on San Juan Island and May promised to pay up. He then went home and killed the old bull which was all the stock he had and loaded this and what furniture he had into two canoes and he and his squaw skipped to Whatcome where he lived for several years as a gambler fleecing the miners who worked the coal mines at that place.

It was while gambling that he acquired the title of "Colonel" by getting a gallon of whiskey and giving everyone a drink who would call him Colonel knowing full well that the name would stick to him in derision but others would come afterward who would think the title genuine. And how many of those sham titles of the west, the Antelope Docs, the Buckskin Joes, the Buffalo Bills, the Mustang Johns, the Apache Joes, the Arapahoe Petes, Comanche Jacks, etc., that I have known have no better origin. May was crafty enough to keep a copy of *Hardee's*

Tactics always on the table. This and his pompous manner easily fooled the groundlings.

The house stood idle for a while, then a Mr. Slaughter and his squaw occupied it while he ran the Lime works. It came next to a Capt. Smith whose house was at Cascade Bay, now Rosario, and from whom it was purchased by Mr. Setzer, including the claim.

It was while "Col." May was at Whatcom that the Fitzhugh incident as it was called occurred and while I give it as the old settlers gave it to me, I can not vouch for its accuracy. Fitzhugh, who claimed to belong to that old Virginia celebrated family, was like "Col." May, living by his wits and a pack of cards. He grew very jealous of another gambler regarding his squaw and shot him. The story says assassinated him, then he used his influence and secured his appointment as Judge of the District and tried and acquitted himself. The story is hardly credible even for those times but I have heard it from several of the old settlers and it is always the same.

"Col." May had returned to the island (Orcas) before my arrival and had located on a claim near North Beach where he had a band of the worst Indian characters always camped under the leadership of an outlaw Indian known as Old Tom to whose credit more than one murder was attributed. Here May posed as the King of Squaw Men, declaring that it was their last ditch (stand) and that he would fight to prevent the settlement of the island by white families, only three of which were on the island at the time; namely, the Setzers, Ephraim Langell from Nova Scotia who married a German servant girl from the mines, and a William Wright from the North of Ireland who had an English wife. These two families were willing to affiliate with the squaw men and it made it very lonesome for Mr. Setzer's people and especially your Mother.

Judge Lewis of the Superior Court had just rendered a decision that all squaw men must marry their squaws or give them one third of their property and send them back to their tribes in a certain time or be punished severely. The feeling ran high among them and they burned the Judge in effigy, and

11

would have murdered him if they had dared. They professed great indignation that they should have to marry squaws though they seemed to think it was all right for them to have families by them.

I was not much surprised when the first Sunday after I had moved into my place "Col." May called to size me up and then proceeded to unload his grievance to find out where I stood. After hinting at the advantage of my getting a half-breed wife who he said would be such a help in opening up a farm, the old wretch by the way was something of a marriage broker in the half-breed market. I heard him through and then said "Mr. May I suppose it's no man's business who you marry, Red, Black or White, but it's every man's business that you (do) marry, not for your sake, for we care nothing about you, but for the poor wretched children that you have brought into the world." That settled it, he marched off with a scowl and I had a bitter, vindictive enemy ever after who certainly did his best to make things hot for me. But this is getting on too fast.

After buying my place and agreeing to take possession on January 1st, 1876, I went to Caines and McLaughlin of the Lime Works to get something to do until that time and the smile on their faces showed what they thought of my ability to do hard work. I had done no manual labor for several years and was just recovering from a severe spell of sickness so I didn't blame them much. They said they had all the men they could use but McLaughlin, in a sneering tone, said that I could cut cordwood at $1.50 a cord. I engaged board at $4.50 a week and bought the implements the last man had used at double their value and set to work. I found out afterward that the regular price per cord was $1.75.

I soon found that I was up against the hardest proposition I had ever met. For the badly twisted timber of these windswept islands is the very hardest wood to cut or split that I have ever seen. So when my first day's work was done and the result was one half cord of wood and ten full sized blisters on my hands and scarcely able to drag my aching bones back to the cookhouse, or to eat after I got there, I began to realize the full beauty of cord wood cutting on Orcas Island for a living. But for the sneers of the old sailor scum who worked at the Lime Works and did not hesitate to say in my presence that they would give the dude as they called me, one week to burn out, I could never have endured it.

I will never forget the next two months. I fell down with vertigo a score of times, but would not give up and I gradually became hardened to it and slowly gained on my daily output until I reached an average 1-1/2 cords per day. I kept that up for a season. So when winter came and those who were going to have me burn out in a week were all discharged and gone, I had about $180 coming to me and was prepared to start work on my own place.

I generally lay around and rested on Sunday or climbed up the mountainside for its glorious view (Mt. Constitution, 2409 feet high) to inspect many new forms of plant life for this region was like a new world to me. I found no pleasure in the sailor scum they often employed at the kiln with whom the greatest blackguard was the best man.

I did go one Sunday with one of the more decent, a Henry Legbandt, to see a claim he had taken up near Doe Bay. The following Sunday he asked me to go to Church with him at the schoolhouse at the head of the Bay. I found as I went along that he wanted to tell me of his troubles; how Miss Brown had refused to go home with him, preferring the company of her brother. He'd show her the next time they met, etc. As it happened we were passing the Adams place and Miss Brown and a Miss Stemenson, a new arrival, were talking at the gate. Henry said "Walk right past and don't notice them", which he did while I stopped and spoke to the ladies for a minute and then went on and overtook (Henry) who was quite sulky about it.

That summer was very dry and hot and I never saw the yellow jackets such pests. I have often been compelled to throw meat away at lunch as they would gather on it in such numbers and sting viciously. Our board got worse toward fall and finally became so bad that the men went on strike led by William

13

Wright who was hauling wood. I warned him against depending on such a lot of men standing together and as I expected they sneaked back to work and Wright was fired. The works were run by Robert M. Caines who represented his stepfather, a Mr. Fowler of Port Townsend and Dan McLaughlin who represented certain parties in Victoria. These two did not get along too well as the works were not a paying proposition and each backer was complaining that the other was not bearing his full share of the loss.

When I came to settle up, knowing that Caines had been doing more than his share and having but little confidence in McLaughlin's honesty, I was just a little anxious about my hard earned money. I waited until I could get together with them and asked for a settlement. They looked over the account, and then McLaughlin cooly told me that they could not pay me. Couldn't pay me a damn cent as he put it. That he was dead broke, etc. I heard him through and asked him for the money again, same answer, but a little more insolent.

I was fast losing patience and control of my temper but I demanded my money again, never speaking to Caines, which showed him that I knew he had been paying more than his share of the bills. Then, what I had hoped for happened. Caines who had sat on the counter swinging his heels and watching us through half closed eyes as usual, straightened up and said "Dan, pay him his money".

"Haven't got a damn cent."

"Pay him anyway."

"I can't."

"Try it."

"I won't."

"Oh yes you will."

"Well, damn it, take it," and he flung a handful of twenties on the counter and Caines settled my account. I always found Caines an honest man and though he drank some in his younger days he settled down into one of San Juan County's best citizens after his marriage with Miss Maggie Douglas of San Juan Island.

3.

These islands were settled largely by former employees of the Hudson's Bay Co. and it was the settled policy of that thrifty company that their employees should all take Indian women for mates. Both that it gave them control of the fur trade of those tribes and it also prevented the tribes from raising against them.

These Indian women were obtained by purchase price ranging from $20 to $50 according to looks and social position in the tribe. Having a Chief's daughter gave a squaw man a fancied superiority over his fellows. Quite a proportion of these women were French Canadian, but there were also a number of Americans both from the North and the South. Then men from the South having left when war threatened and like southerners everywhere they were inveterate office seekers. But to do them justice they generally made good officials.

The most prominent Southerners on our island were J.H. Bowers and John Gray. Judge Bowman did not ever become a squaw man. While Wesley Whitner of Blakely Island and Edward Warbass of San Juan Island made up four very good men who were seldom out of office and did much toward the organization of our county and the only orderly management of its affairs during its earlier years.

Among the French Canadian squaw men were Yoots, the Cayous, the Largins, the Berries, etc.; and a number of their married half-breed children such as the LaPlantes, the Freshettes, the Bulls, etc. Among the squaw men were Shattuck, Stevens, Adams, "Col." May, Trustworthy, Brown, Clark, Moore, Vierick, Smith, Guthrie, Hitchens, Legbandt, Robinson, Boos, Bratton, Bridges, etc.

15

My first Christmas on the island was rather a lonely one as I had made no acquaintances and books and papers were not to be had at all. I was amused at the manner in which Caines and Billy O'Donnell were celebrating it. They had a jug of whiskey and a box of crackers and they sat astride a bench and first one and then the other had to tell a story or sing a song and the other would treat, or vice versa and they kept this up till both of them fell into a drunken slumber.

This reminds me of the following Christmas when Joe Bridges and his squaw and Tilton Sheets, our surveyor, came home to Langdon from San Juan Town loaded with booze and landed their boat on the beach where the water was the deepest and Bridges and the squaw Betsy got ashore all right but Sheets got turned around the wrong way and walked out over the stern of the boat into deep water. They fished him out and helped him up to Bridges' cabin and got him into dry clothes, but in trying to change his nether garments he stumbled and sat down in the big basket in which the squaw kept her fancy glassware and Betsy letting out a stream of Chinook Billingsgate, seized a broom and began beating him. Poor Sheets, who could neither get the garment off nor on, hopped out the door amid the shouts and laughter of the crowd which the squaw's screams had collected. This Tilton Sheets was the man who surveyed our island and when sober, was not only a skillful surveyor, but also a man of more than ordinary intelligence. But his intemperate habits made him in a few years a complete wreck and caused his early death by delirium tremens.

There was at this time no store on the island except the few things kept by Caines and McLaughlin for their men. There had been some years previously a small Indian trading post kept at a place called Grindstone Bay by a man named Paul K. Hubbs, a man who, coming from a good family had so degenerated that he gloried in the name of a white Indian and was looked upon with contempt by the very Indians themselves.

The settlers on the island at that time did their trading either by smuggling their goods from Victoria or trading with Israel Katz, a merchant of San Juan Town whose policy was to get his

16

customers started drinking by generously treating them to his vile liquor when they arrived. Then, when they were half drunk, selling them far more than they intended to buy. Then when settling-up time came in the fall and they were unable to pay, he always said "That's all right. Just give me a little note and let it run."

As soon as they acquired title to their lands he got them to secure their notes by mortgage, saying that "it was a mere matter of form. You know Katz will never crowd you." The natural result was that Katz soon became a large landowner.

The methods of farming were extremely crude and most of the work was done with oxen. The carts were used in lieu of wagons and were made by boring a hole in a large fir log in the center for the axle and having wooden wheels made by sawing a slice of the same log and sliding the hole made onto the axle and fastening it with a wooden pin. But these carts were only owned by the well-to-do. Others contented themselves with a crude sled with wooden runners made by bending a fir pole and pinning it to the framework. Dragging this sled on bare ground with an ox team over rocky trails was slow work and tedious compared to the automobile and the fine highways of the present. But we blazed the way for others to travel.

In September the Republican Primaries were held and I went up to the schoolhouse at the head of the Bay to see how things were managed. Not having been in the Territory a year I had no vote. "Col." May as the Republican boss called the meeting to order and without electing a chairman, or voting at all he simply appointed Charles Shattuck and James Stevens, two of his squaw men, as delegates and told them what he wanted them to do and that was all there was to it.

When it was over I asked one of them if that was the usual performance. He said it was, that the "Colonel" attended to everything. I said if that was the case I think I will take a hand and see if we can't have a new deal, for I don't believe in stacking the cards in that manner. He looked at me as though I were crazy and maybe I did look so to him. But I resolved to break up that, and the next Primary I made it my business to

17

get acquainted with all the more honest squaw men to get them to promise to attend and conduct the Primary in an honest manner.

Of course this was all reported to "Col." May and I expected there would be a stormy time. But when the day arrived and we gathered at the schoolhouse we found it locked and none of May's crowd there. After waiting till the time was past for the Primary I asked them to come with me to Shattuck's store, he being the school clerk. I asked Shattuck why the schoolhouse was not open at two o'clock for the Primary. He pretended to be surprised and asked "What Primary?" I meant. "Oh," he said, "that was all over some time ago." I asked him how and he said that the "Colonel" got the boys together at ten a.m. and held it. I told him that he knew well that the Republican Primary was to be held at two p.m.

I stepped over to him and said, "Shattuck, give me the keys to the schoolhouse." He hesitated but saw that I was going to hit him and gave them up.

We then went to the schoolhouse and held our Primary in the proper manner. They chose me as chairman and wanted to send me as one of the delegates, but I declined as I thought it better that two of the older settlers should go. I knew that May would claim that this greenhorn, as he called me, wanted to shove the old settlers back and run things themselves. So we chose two good men and sent them to the convention carefully instructing them to work for the interests of the island.

But "Col." May's influence was so great as the self-styled king of the squaw men that the convention dared not refuse seats to our duly elected delegates. They allowed his also and Orcas Island had double representation. This was the beginning of my political fight with May and I never quit until I had him completely eliminated. But this is again taking a long look ahead.

On January 1, 1876, I took possession of my place and as Mr. Setzer was not ready to move I lived with them in the meantime and had a good opportunity to get acquainted with your Mother. The result of which was that I persuaded her to

18

The Tulloch Farm at the foot of Mt. Constitution on Orcas Island. The year was 1903.

Gordon Keith

A portion of the James Francis Tulloch farm as it appears today. The house is at the far left, and the pond, where the fishing wharf was, can be seen in the foreground.

promise to come back in September and help me make a home of it. I afterwards succeeded in shortening the time to June 21st.

I bought a ton of seed potatoes from Wm. O'Donnell who had bought what afterward was the "Bostian Place" and pitted them near the house and fenced it in. But a pig belonging to Mr. Setzer took a special delight in breaking down the fence and scuttling the pit. I drove it off a number of times and was fast losing my temper to the delight of your Mother's little sisters.

Finally, when they came again with the report that the pig was in the pit I seized a rock and with an oath I fear, I took the top of its head off for I was always a good shot with a rock or gun. I offered to pay for it as I supposed I had killed it, but Mrs. Setzer said I had done just right. It did not die and was a part of our wedding dinner. A few days later my chickens started scratching up my garden and wore my patience out so I threw a rock at one of them and took its head off. I was really afraid that these exhibitions of temper would prejudice your Mother against me but it seems that it did not.

After they had moved away in March (Setzers) I had a somewhat similar experience. I was working at William Wright's across the Bay exchanging work for the team work and coming home five miles on Wednesday and Saturday to look after things. I had the acre in front planted in potatoes and when I got home one evening I found an old sow of Sam Brown's scuttling my potatoes. I drove her out and fixed the fence and went on down to the Lime kiln for my mail. When I got back, tired out, I saw the wretched brute busy at work again. I opened the gate and tried to drive her out but she would run right past the open gate and begin tearing up the potatoes so I went inside and got my pistol. Thinking to scare her off, I fired over her but she paid no attention and losing my temper I said "Then damn it, take this".

It was a long shot and although it was almost dark I could see between me and the water. When she dropped I didn't even go to see her but went in and threw myself on the bed dressed as I was and slept. In the morning she was gone, but following the trail of blood I found her in my roothouse shot through the shoulder. I went to see Brown on my way to Wright's, to settle with him, but he was gone and his squaw "Old Sally" who couldn't speak a word of English still understood that I was complaining of the sow. She got a club and pounded on the ground and said "Sow, Sow", thus showing me what to do.

I said nothing about this to Wright till Saturday afternoon, for I did not trust him; but I told him then as I could see Brown on my way home. Wright heard me and said "you've killed it and buried it?" Evidently thinking he had a hold over me. He was disappointed when I told him I was going to pay Brown that night. When I saw Brown he said it had served the damn thing right and offered to call the whole thing square for the harm the sow had done. But I paid him $5 for her, and she raised me a fine litter of pigs afterward. I had a good deal to do with William Wright and found him rather untrustworthy.

Miss Brown (later Tulloch's wife) had taught school the year before I arrived. The scholars were half-breeds whose main characteristic seemed to be stolidity and sulkiness. But this summer there was no school whatever, and as I needed some supplies, I went to Port Townsend for them. May, being on the same boat, proposed that I should do my trading with Rothschild or the Baron as he called himself. So I went with him and was introduced. This D.C.H. Rothschild, or the Baron as his friends called him, was something of a character. He had the principal ship candlery in Port Townsend which was the port of entry and chief outfitting point for the shipping of Puget Sound.

His was also one of the chief supply houses for the extensive lumber and logging interests of the Sound. A great many loggers made his firm their bankers also, as he had succeeded in gaining their confidence. Having on hand a large stock of shelf-worn misfit goods that he wanted to get rid of so he could stock up fresh, he gave out the word that he was broke and when the poor fellows who had deposited with him came, he wrung his hands and bemoaned his hard luck. He told them that the Old Baron would strip himself of his last cent to pay what he could, "so go right ahead, boys, and help yourself to whatever you want at cost price." And the poor fellows, thinking half a loaf better than none, cleaned his shelves for him at what he called half or cost price. The old rascal, who had his agent in Frisco laying in a new stock, wired him to ship it and Rothschild bloomed again.

When "Col." May turned me over to him I was afraid he was going to kiss me. But I got what I required and his promise that he would ship me whatever I ordered, "and pay for it yust ven effer you feels like it."

May had to get some things for Sam Brown including two cases of the best coaloil. These things were placed with mine and as I stood reading the paper, but keeping an eye on things, I saw old Rothschild order a clerk to change the oil and replace it with an inferior and cheaper brand. When May came around I informed him of this and when he went after the old rascal you'd have thought he was going to cry. "It vas all dat stupid clerk's doing", and he'd have to discharge him sure.

I got about $35 worth from him during the summer and as money I had expected from Bismark failed to come, it cramped me badly and I was not able to pay just when I intended to. Old Rothschild began writing me some threatening letters, dunning me every week. I answered a few of them, telling him just how I was fixed and then I quit replying to them. I felt sure that old "Col." May was egging him on, but finally Bob Caines, who had just returned from Port Townsend, handed me a letter which said the old Baron had asked him to give me. It was another dun and closed with: "If you cannot pay me, at least answer my letters".

I answered at once as follows: "Mr.D.C.H. Rothschild, Will you please go to hell. Very truly yours, James F. Tulloch." By return mail I got the sweetest letter I have ever received. It was all a mistake of his correspondence clerk, just take my time and if there was anything I wanted, just send for it. I never answered, but paid him up as soon as I could. The old fraud shot himself on the beach some years after.

While returning on the little steamer "Teaser" from Port Townsend, we had to sleep on the floor and were suddenly wakened by the vessel turning over on her side. As we supposed

22

that we were out in the straits and that she was going down, the passengers were scrambling up from the floor like rats, myself included. I tried to open the door only to be laughed at by the Captain and crew. We had crossed the straits while we slept and had run aground at Lopez and the tide had run out causing our boat to drop over on her side, giving us a good scare.

4.

My first farming was to dig up an acre in front with a mattock and plant potatoes. This ground was on old Indian village located here on account of the stream, the harbor and the clams. One place was shown to me where 23 Indians were surprised and killed by one of the northern tribes. These northern Indians were far more war-like than the Sound Indians whom they contemptuously styled 'Sap a lalo' or bread eaters. I dug up many skeletons in this tract, one of which had the arrow head still in a rib.

The little islands on the north side of the harbor were a burying ground for these tribes whose custom it was to put the dead in their own canoes and place it among the branches of the scrub Juniper trees that grew there. A log that lay on the point north of the harbor had its limbs lopped off and each decorated with a human skull of which there were over a score.

The 21st of June, the time set for our marriage having arrived, Henry Stone, Wallace Wardell and I decided on a hunt as a goodbye to bachelorhood. So we started at daybreak and pulled across the Bay and skirted the west shore to the White beach but with no success. While rowing along we saw below the boat a fine specimen of the wolf fish. When we struck it with an oar it seized our oar viciously. It was probably 6-7 feet long with a head that seemed to us to almost resemble a bull-dog.

Wardell said, "Boys, leave this to me to tell at the wedding and see if Mike Adams doesn't out-lie me." We knew that Adams would be at the wedding and we knew his record as a spinner of tall tales. So when Wardell told the assembled guests of our hairbreadth escape from the horrid monster which he described as a cross between a Chinese Daagob and a sea serpent and about 40 feet long, Adams said: "Yes, that's it exactly. We killed one at the mouth of the Stikine, but it was over 50 feet long."

We ran across from White Beach to Stockade Bay and got Judge Bowman to perform the ceremony and stopped at Langdon for Bob Caines, these three being my invited guests. When we arrived we found assembled Mr. and Mrs. E. Langell, Mr. and Mrs. Wright, Miss Stevenson, Mrs. Harry McKeen from Point Roberts, a Mr. Ayers from the mainland and Adams, Shattuck and Allen Robinson. I was none too well pleased seeing those squaw men there, but Mr. Setzer had business dealings with them and didn't want to offend them.

Mr. Setzer and I, while differing on politics, religion and most everything else, got along fairly well for I knew that he was a good honest man and was as good to your Mother as though he had been her own Father. In fact, he made no distinction whatever between her and his own children. Your grandmother Setzer was always one of my best friends.

These squaw men were the worst scandalmongers and mischief makers I have ever seen and those four, May, Adams, Shattuck and Robinson, were the worst of the lot. They used to gather every Sunday, first at one place, then at another, and everyone tried to be present as they knew that the absent one would be torn to pieces. After I succeeded in getting a few white families in, they started the most terrible stories about them—stories without a shred of truth. But these old squaw men were natural blackguards and seemed to gloat in filthy stories.

I suppose we did not escape, but we had as little as possible to do with them so we knew nothing of it. I was amused at their efforts to find out if I was calling on your Mother during our engagement. One of them went to Mr. Setzer to find out if "that young fellow was coming to see Miss Brown". Mr. Setzer drawled out: "Well, he isn't coming to see me."

One Sunday as I was on my way to the Setzers, the squaw men were gathered in front of Adams as usual. Adams actually followed me for a couple of miles to find out where I was going. So I gave him a run for his money by going a few miles out of my way and fooling him.

They certainly were a queer lot, but I wish to be just to these people, for with the exception of "Col." May, they were fairly honest and were hospitable in their homes. But for having intermingled with the Indians they might have been very good average people.

There were a few, such as John Grey, William Moore and the French Canadians and some of the half-breeds, who were in all respects good citizens. But while it is hard indeed for the savage to become civilized, it is easy for the civilized to become a savage.

After our marriage we settled down to the hard task of gaining a livlihood under the most adverse conditions, for we had no team and I had to change work with Wright, giving him two days for one. While I was working there I could only come home twice a week, owing to the long distance. I have since learned that your Mother suffered greatly from fear of the Indians that were often camped on our beach. She would not tell me of it at the time as she knew that we had to have the team work; and as the Indians were relations of the white men's squaws, they were all peaceable. But a young girl could not think of this and she suffered for it. Had she told me, I certainly would have abandoned the place and gone to town. I've often regretted that I did not anyhow as I could have developed a far more full and pleasant life there for both of us. I sized myself up with other men in business enough to know that I could have held my own. I never took kindly to the life of a farmer, its loneliness and isolation made it always repugnant to me.

Our mailboat, the little "Teaser" was little more than coffin-size and made weekly trips when the weather was favorable. A trip on her was nothing to be desired when crossing our stormy straits.

26

While "Col." May was the worst smuggler on the island, he was not the only one by any means, for smuggling seemed to be one of the main industries. The chief contraband articles being opium, wool and Chinese. The price of wool on the Canadian side being about half that paid on our side made raising wool on a foggy night extremely profitable and J.L. Sherer, our county auditor who made a careful canvas, found that the yearly yield of San Juan County was 27 lbs., while the actual clip was 2-1/2 lbs. But this kind of smuggling was considered eminently respectable and was indulged in extensively by some of our county officials, including a Commissioner of the County from San Juan Island who, being a sheep raiser, carried on this illicit trade continually. But the smuggling of opium and Chinese was considered to be of a somewhat shady character of business and only indulged in by men of the "Col." May and Kelly class.

This Kelly who lived on a neighboring island was one of the most desperate of the opium and Chinese smugglers and though repeatedly caught and convicted, continued to smuggle while out of jail as long as he lived. It was claimed by his friends that on one of his trips with a load of Chinese he was fast being overhauled by a revenue cutter and he killed the Chinese and threw them overboard then let himself be overhauled and examined. This I cannot vouch for, but it is quite in keeping with the man's character.

Recognizing the need for water on my shell beach land I decided to try and turn part of the stream and carry it along the hillside and above the house and on to the garden. Mr. Setzer said it could not be done, but having made a water level no spirit level to be had, I found that there was a fall enough. So digging my ditch around stumps and around logs and even under them, I soon had a fine stream flowing above the house. Aside from its value for irrigation, it became a great convenience for your Mother; that is, until Ross became old enough to crawl to it, when it became a nightmare.

When we planted our rose garden with 75 different kinds of ever-blooming roses we began to take pride in our place and dreamed of what we would make of it in years to come. I had

27

planted a quantity of strawberry plants which, in that rich soil, and with abundance of water, yielded enormously. However, our potatoes in the valley behind, owing to the land being undrained, were smothered in chickenweed. We soon saw that our hopes of a crop had gone a glimmering.

Towards fall we went down to Lopez Island to do some trading at Hutchinson's store. This Hutchinson, or Hutch as he was called, was a single man from New England who, with his sister, Mrs. Weeks, kept the only store on that island. He had a kind heart, but an abusive tongue and he certainly had cause to use it, for those lazy squaw men broke him up in business. He could not refuse them credit though he knew he'd never get his pay. If they came to him with a story of hungry squaws and children at home, he couldn't resist their pleas.

While we were there we glanced out and saw one of those cultus characters landing his canoe and exclaimed, "There comes that. . ., but he won't get a darn thing here. He's owed me for four years and he won't work, etc." The fellow came in and said, "Hutch, I want some flour and bacon and sugar, my family are out of everything. I'll pay you soon." All right, Hutch said, and gave him the supplies and when he had gone he turned loose on him at a fearful rate. How he ever held out as long as he did surprised me for he was imposed upon shamefully. But I'd rather take my chances in the sweet by and by with such as he than with all the sanctimonious ones that ever filled the Amen corner.

On the way down we stopped at Yott's Landing for a time and as it was cold, Stevens, who ran the boat, asked us to go up to the house some distance from the landing. We found Mr. Yott sitting in front of his fireplace in his stocking feet and shirt-sleeves contentedly smoking while his squaw went about her household duties in her bare feet and dressed seemingly in one calico garment. Presently Gifford, who had been elected Justice of the Peace, arrived to marry them, for they had learned that the law must be complied with. They both stood up just as they were, except that Yott took his pipe out of his mouth long enough to make the responses. Then he went on smoking

Left to right: Isabel, Ida, Mrs. Annie Tulloch, Laura and Eva Tulloch. This photo was taken at the Tulloch farm on Orcas Island in 1903.

and she resumed her work. It sure was a strange wedding. These people were French Canadians and their children were all grown up and several had families, altogether they were among the most peaceful law abiding residents on the island.

I paid Hutchinson the next year in potatoes at $2.75 per ton and he said that I was the only one who had paid up that fall. I hate to think or remember about the hardships and privations your Mother had to go through and yet she never complained. It's no wonder that I have always said a better wife and Mother never lived.

29

5.

The deer were a great pest. We had a fine cabbage patch close to the house but in spite of its closeness, the deer were destroying it. As I could not work all day and watch all night, I determined to try setting a gun. I pointed my rifle at about the height of my knees, but I feared that would be too low.

We were awakened by the shot about midnight and I found the deer struggling on the ground. I struck it a couple of blows on the head with an axe and thinking that I had put it out of its misery, I went back to bed. But the next morning my deer was gone, leaving a trail where it had dragged itself toward the Bay. I found it by the front fence with its back broken. So, instead of my rifle being aimed too low, I came within an inch of overshooting it.

The first deer I killed on the island I shot with a spade. I was doing some ditch digging in the field behind and while going out to work I heard the dogs from the Lime kiln chasing a deer on the trail that I knew crossed mine a short distance ahead. The trail passed under a log so I stationed myself beside the log and as the deer dodged under it, I struck it on the head with the edge of the spade. So I really did shoot my first deer with a spade.

They were terrible pests and we had to resort to every possible device to get rid of them. Our chief methods were setting guns, setting stakes, still hunting and fire hunting. One man hunting with a fire jack killed five in one evening. But the luckiest shooting I ever did was some years later when the deer were digging up my potatoes worse than usual. They pawed the potatoes out, then ate them, very often destroying the whole crop. So I got a number of buckshot cartridges for my shotgun and as I had to hunt at early daybreak, for the deer always leave before it gets light, I posted myself carefully on the log fence and waited for them at dawn. Finally, fancying that I saw something moving among the ferns, I fired and two other deer ran for the fence. I fired at each in quick succession, but the light was so poor I had little hope of having hit any of them. But on going to where I had fired at the first one, I found my deer all right, and I found the next one I had shot at but found no trace of the third.

I thought this pretty good shooting in the dark, but what was my surprise when I came to skin them I found them peppered with birdshot. In my haste I had taken birdshot instead of buckshot cartridges. And to add to it, your Mother found the other carcass accidentally a few days after. It was also killed with birdshot. I have been loath to tell this often because so few believe it, but your Mother knows it to be the truth. In fact, one stands a much better chance of being believed if he tells preposterous impossible yarns than if he tells the actual truth.

This reminds me of a time when I was track laying on the Cairo and Fulton in Arkansas. I was speaking in the manner in which we killed horn toads with our whips and the way the owls, rattlesnakes and prairie dogs all roomed together, when a Black Irishman told me he'd heard just enough damned lies about toads with horns and owls and rattlesnakes and prairie dogs living together. That no one but a damned fool would believe such a lie. He had the whole crowd with him and I was put in the Annanias class at once.

After harvesting my very lean crop that only netted me $45 I began cutting wood for the Lime kiln on the hill near Cascade Lake and as the weather was very stormy I caught a severe cold which settled in my lungs and put me in a very bad way. But Shattuck's squaw saw me suffering from hemorrhage of the lungs and gave me some of the seeds that the Indians use for consumption and they gave me almost immediate relief. These seeds which are very pungent and aromatic grow on a little island near Eastsound and certainly have great merit.

31

I succeeded in getting my debts paid and devoted the winter to clearing land and draining what was already cleared. Orcas Island was visited nearly every winter by one or more terrific snowstorms from the Northeast, which drifted the snow so deep that the roads were impassable and though it rarely went below freezing, still, in that moist climate we felt the cold worse than the same degree in the drier climates of the East. Fortunately these blizzards only lasted a few days at a time. The islands, owing to their exposed position, are always very windy, which makes the catarrah trouble very common.

Orcas Island being quite mountainous was largely devoted to sheep raising by the early settlers who each claimed certain portions of the island as their range. Sheep thief was quite a common term to fling at each other. But local stealings were small compared to the exploits of certain enterprising citizens of Victoria who often made forays and with the aid of trained sheep dogs rounded up whole boat loads on moonlight nights. One family is said to have done a thriving business in this line.

During the summer a very sad accident occurred at point Langdon Lime works. The two little half-breed children of George Phillips who had married the Fitzhugh squaw found the storeroom and went into it and unscrewed the top off a powder can and dropped a lighted match into it causing them both a horrible death from inhaling the flames.

It was shortly before this that "Col." May and Phillips put up a job to swindle a poor French logger that they knew had some ready money. "Col." May invited him to his home and pretended to be not only a "Colonel" but a very pious Catholic. He made the Frenchman believe that he was keeping company with the very elect. He made him believe that to be received among the very best families he must be a sport and must keep up a front. He must get a gold watch, a game dog and a gun. And he told (the Frenchman) that he knew just where the very watch he needed was. He said that it was an heirloom and the man would not part with it except for its full value. He told the man that if he could get that watch and a gold chain that his

32

friend Phillips had that used to belong to his Mother, that he'd look like a sport for sure.

So "Col." May went to Port Townsend and got an Oriode watch and chain costing $4. He gave them to Phillips who parted with them almost in tears. Thus they succeeded in robbing the poor fool of some $200. Not content with that, they picked up a mangy cur dog and an old dollar gun and unloaded them on the Frenchman at an awful price.

God knows what their next swindle would have been if Bob Caines had not asked me to go with him and show the thing up. We had some difficulty in convincing the Frenchman that he had been fleeced, but his indignation was great when we gave him proof of it.

"Why I would have been on my guard," he said, "if it had been anyone else, but the "Colonel" had Jesus Christ hung up all over his house. And then to cheat a poor working man."

All dances at this time were squaw dances to which only Mrs. Wright of the white women went, and she went only for trade reasons. But later on the half-breed girls, some of whom were fairly good looking, made the squaws play wallflowers. And when finally the white families came in, the half-breeds had to take a back seat or have separate dances.

We were amused at this time over the account of a squaw ball at Eastsound schoolhouse, at which Mr. Wright and wife were present. Wright for trade reasons had brought along a good supply of the black current wine primed with alcohol that he manufactured that year. He was doing a custom house business until the crowd got so drunk that Mr. Wright, fearing public opinion, declared, "William, I'll never make another drop as long as I live." And Wright, with a tipsy leer replied, "Weel, Louisey, I dinna care a dom, I can mak it maself."

On August 7th, 1877 Ross was born and your Mother naturally thought there never was such a baby. Wishing to be a model husband and have no discord in the family I heartily agreed with her. Mrs. Zeigler who had located at the head of the Bay acted in the character of a midwife on the occasion and insisted that I should get some whiskey. But in mixing the toddy she made the mistake of using salt instead of sugar and when your Mother refused to touch the stuff Mrs. Zeigler, who had conscientious scruples against any kind of waste, at once declared that whiskey, with salt or without, was whiskey and she drank it eagerly and all was well.

I planted 300 apple trees that fall as the beginning of my south orchard and I remember thinking when the snow was on the ground that winter and those little switches were sticking up in rows that it was a long look ahead to imagine myself harvesting a crop of apples from them.

That fall "Col." May went to Port Townsend and got some forty or more people from that place to sign as residents of Waldron Island for his petition for a post office on Waldron Island. The island had a half dozen squaw men on it, but with his forged petition it was promptly granted. When the bids were called, May being the only one (bidding) got it at a very high price. He then sublet it and got the lion's share for doing nothing. Having carried through this scheme so successfully he induced a tool of his, a squaw man named Viereck, who lived at Doe Bay to try the same game in our neighborhood. But in this game I took a hand and though this occurred a year or two afterward, I may as well mention it here.

Hearing of the proposed scheme I met Viereck one day and told him that I had been informed that he had made an application for a post office at Doe Bay through a forged petition, using Port Townsend names, as "Col." May had done on Waldron Island. I told him that while I'd like to see Doe Bay (on Orcas Island) get the post office, still, if he tried any swindling games here he'd find that he was not the only bidder for the mail contract.

But Viereck thought I was bluffing and laughed at me. When the bids were called for I figured carefully just what I could (carry the mail for) without actual loss. As one dollar a day was the average wage, I put in my bid at $150 a year, for weekly service, or three dollars per day for myself and pony.

Viereck, like May, thought he'd have it all to himself, put in a bid, if I remember right, for $1700. He was raging when he

34

heard that I put one in and made all kinds of threats. The Postmaster General wrote to our County Auditor to see what it meant that there was such a difference in the bids. He (also) inquired as to my standing in the community and my ability to fill the contract. The Judge wrote back that I was the best and that he and the Treasurer would willingly go on my bond, and that the other bid was an attempted swindle. So my bid was accepted and I went to Seattle and bought a pony and saddle, paying $37 for them.

When I began the service I found that Viereck, who was postmaster at Doe Bay, had arranged the schedule to suit himself by beginning (the route) at Doe Bay instead of at Eastsound where the mail landed. He boasted that he'd make it cost me two days every week. I wrote Washington at once, showing the facts in the case and got my order changing the schedule and upon delivering the mail and requesting the sack for the return trip, Viereck being absent, (his helper) refused, but upon my threat to report him he yielded. On my next trip Peter Morris, at whose place I always stopped for dinner, met me and asked me if I was heeled as Viereck had sworn he would shoot me. I told him that it was careless of me not to have taken out life insurance, but I guessed that I'd go back for dinner, as men who carried so many pistols seldom were very dangerous.

When I turned over the mail Viereck was very civil and invited me to dinner and the worst he ever did to me was to have a great deal of patent reports come during the stormy weather of winter when I had to carry my load on foot. When my term was up I told him I was not going to bid again (for the contract) but he did not believe me and put in a very reasonable bid and got it.

6.

It was the year following that the murder of George Phillips by his squaw occurred at Point Langdon Lime Works. I had witnessed some trouble between Phillips and his squaw a few days before while they were passing my place in their canoe. The quarrel ended by the squaw striking him on the head with a paddle and it was no love tap either.

But this day his stepson Mason Fitzhugh came hurrying past my place and called to me to go down to Langdon and keep the hogs away from Phillips' body while he went for the coroner. I found (Phillips) on the trail between the cookhouse and his residence and went to get his squaw to help me carry him in. But she would not and kept on with her washing as though nothing had happened. So I waited till Mason came with the coroner and jurors.

When we made a careful examination of the body while preparing it for burial, we knew we'd be called as witnesses. It developed that Phillips wanted his stepson Mason Fitzhugh, who was the son of Fitzhugh of Whatcom, who tried and acquitted himself of murder, to marry a sister of Joseph Bull, but the squaw with a natural jealousy of her race, thought that Phillips was like John Alden, speaking for himself, and lay for him with a shotgun, both charges entering his neck and breast and causing almost instant death.

The squaw was sent to Port Townsend prison and gave birth to a child while there. When the trial came she was given two years minus time already served. She was defended by C.M. Bradshaw, a former squaw man, but who now had a white family. His plea was solely one of sentiment as the facts proved it simply a cooly planned assassination. In giving my evidence and in describing the body as we found it I testified that some of the shot had passed almost through the body and lay against the skin, which was true.

After the trial I heard some of the jurors discussing it and referring to it as a lie, declaring it was impossible to shoot through a man's body. I do not like our jury system for with our court rules, excepting for cause and without it, we too often succeed in eliminating all but the unfit.

William B. Warren, or Charlie Warren as we called him, sent me the money from Bismark to buy him a claim as his term of enlistment would be out in a year or so. I bought him the claim that was later known as the Jorgenson place for which I paid $280. Charlie came out the next year and made his home with us for some time. We exchanged work and drained his marshland and put in a crop of potatoes which yielded well but the pesky deer harvested them for us.

We had very hard times on the Sound those years. There was practically no flour to be had. The Sweeney Bros. who had a little store where Orcas is now had a couple barrels which they held at $13 and as potatoes were $3 per ton, there naturally was but little flour bought. Wages were $1 per day when any work could be obtained. So Charlie and I took a contract to cut cordwood at Coon Harbor for the Lime Works, but as it had to be cut on cut-over land, we found it very slow and hard work. We had to throw it down the bank and cord it on the beach. I do not believe we averaged fifty cents a day each.

Charlie stuck to his place for a few years but the squaw men got after him, knowing he would not take a squaw and discouraged him. So, in spite of all I could do, he sold out for a song and went to Seattle where I lost sight of him.

Jorgenson sold a fourth of the claim to a man named Wiggins, a squaw man from Sucia Island and later he sold off the balance for $6000. I was vexed to see Charlie lose his place as I knew it would be quite valuable after a while. Besides, Warren was a friend of ours.

The Sweeneys were former loggers from Wisconsin and their store on Orcas Island soon became an eyesore, for they dealt as much in wet goods as dry. The place soon became pandemonium. Joe Sweeney went afterward to Friday Harbor where he opened a store in partnership with Izett, the custom house collector. This was a very convenient arrangement as Steven Sweeney, the younger brother, was running a trading boat to Victoria and as smuggling was one of the main industries of most boatmen in those days, it was very convenient to know just where the customs officer was at all times.

I bought fifty leghorn chickens the second year and made it pay well, but I made the common mistake of raising 500 the next year and went broke. I next tried hog raising but the price paid for pork was so low that I gave it up. In fact, there was nothing one could raise that would pay but apples and that for me was a dream of the future, though I still kept planting our trees and caring for them. Finding that the cost of nursery stock was too great and the quality too poor, I established my own nursery and not only raised my own trees, but had a quantity for sale.

It was about this time that I offered Sam Brown, whose pig I had shot, $100 for the secret of how he made his living, provided it was honest. I am certain that he was passing counterfeit money, quantities of which were in circulation. Brown was always flush with money and never did any work. Our islands had been a no-man's land for so long that such characters flocked to them.

We had two people drown nearby and in both cases it was from intoxication. William Harrod and Tilton Sheets pulled past our place one day, both full of booze and singing. Just above our little island Harrod fell overboard and though we grappled all afternoon for his body, we failed to find it. Shortly afterward Capt. Smith, from whom Mr. Setzer bought our place, started home from Eastsound drunk and his body was found washed up on Langell's beach the next day. But in all the 35 years I lived on Orcas Island I never heard of a sober person drowning.

While sitting on our porch one evening we saw a large meteorite dart across the heavens from a northerly direction and plunge into the Bay. This was the only really large meteorite I ever saw fall, though I saw a fine one near Dale City that had fallen there sometime in the past. It was pitted and glazed on its surface by fusion while passing through the atmosphere and was nearly round and about a foot in diameter and extremely heavy. Evidently it was composed of iron and nickel as so many of them are. It was, in short, a little globe in space pulled down to our earth by its greater attraction, after having whirled through space for countless ages. I have often regretted not having secured this specimen, as those who found it simply thought it a chunk of iron.

The Captain of our mail steamer during the '80's was Herbert Beecher, a son of Henry Ward Beecher, the famous Pastor of Plymouth Church. He was often referred to as "Beecher's bad boy". But though he was wild he was a good seaman and personally I had no fault to find with him. He was always courteous and honest in his dealings with me. He even went out of his way at times to do me a kindness. I think it likely that much of the evil report regarding him was due to his outspoken contempt for squawmen. It was while Beecher was here that the Lucy Bean swindle was carried out by "Col." May and some of his gang on the little islands off the Gulf of Georgia.

Bill Bean was a despicable character whose means of support was smuggling. He had no squaw or children so we were surprised at seeing our mails at Eastsound loaded with letters to a Miss Lucy Bean, care of "Colonel" S. May. We knew that there was some rascality afoot. When dozens of boxes and bales of merchandise began arriving for the same party, it seemed time that something was done about it.

Luckily, one of our people got a paper from his Eastern home which explained it all, as it contained a letter from Miss Lucy Bean. The letter said that Lucy Bean was a little white girl on an island out in the Gulf of Georgia whose Father was a missionary who had been murdered by the Indians. She wanted to build a church and teach the Indian children there to worship God, the Father of all, etc. It was the most blasphem-

39

ous piece of scoundrelism I ever saw. It was well adapted to loosen the purse strings of Eastern women.

In closing, after appealing for an organ for her church and a knitting machine to knit socks for the little heathens, she pleaded her extreme poverty and implored all to enclose one dollar. In return, she would send them clam shells and oyster shells. The letter brought them several organs and knitting machines which they then sold in Victoria.

Shattuck, our postmaster, when shown this, refused to do anything though every mail brought hundreds of letters. He turned them over to "Col." May and called it a smart trick of the "Colonel's". But Beecher positively refused to carry the freight and May had to get it from Port Townsend by other means.

We wrote to the Eastern papers and exposed the swindle. But as this took time, the rascals reaped a rich harvest. Such rascality only increased our determination to get in white families from the East as speedily as possible. I then called the few white families we had to meet at our house and we organized the Orcas Island Improvement Association, of which I asked to be the secretary, corresponding secretary and treasurer. We made Peter Bostian chairman but he simply was a figurehead.

Having all put up our due share of the necessary funds, they went home and left me to run it. This I proceeded to do by getting up a circular that described our islands as rose colored as the facts would warrant, showing their great advantage in location, climate, soil and products. I struck off 7000 circulars and through acquaintances at Whatcom, Port Townsend, Seattle and Tacoma, I got agents to meet all incoming trains and vessels and distribute them.

I also began a systematic correspondence with Eastern papers and here my former dealings with them while in Bismark helped me greatly as it gave me editorial endorsement. The results were soon evident, for Orcas Island had a veritable settler's boom.

Although "May" and his squaw men did all they could to discourage new arrivals, we were soon in a position to change

Eastsound's Emmanuel Episcopal Church in the 1800's, long before the Parish Hall had been added to it.

Templin family photo

Steamboats, a part of Puget Sound's "Mosquito Fleet," are tied up at Eastsound on Orcas Island. In the foreground is Harrison dock at Arbutus Point (Madrona Point). In the background is Templin's dock. The two structures adjacent to the dock are Templin's Fair and Emmanuel Episcopal Church.

In the Name of the Father, and of the Son,
and of the Holy Ghost. Amen.

THIS CERTIFIES THAT

Eva Irene Tulloch

RECEIVED

✠ Holy Baptism ✠

in *Emmanuel Church*
East Sound

Diocese of *Washington*

on the *7th Sunday after Trinity being*
the *8th* day of *August*

IN THE YEAR OF OUR LORD 18*86*

Parents { *James Tulloch.*
Nancy Ann Tulloch.

Sponsors { *Rev. S.R.S. Gray.*

or { *Mrs. A. Gray.*

Witnesses { *Mrs. J.E. Hambly.*
S.R.S. Gray.

Recorded Parish Register No. *1* Page *8*

A facsimile of the original baptismal certificate of Eva Irene Tulloch, signed by
S.R.S. Gray and dated August 8, 1886, one year after Emmanuel Church opened
its doors for services.

social matters and Orcas Island began to be known as one of the most progressive sections of the Sound country.

Shortly after this we had a visit from three gentlemen who introduced themselves as Dr. Nevins, the Episcopal Minister of Olympia, Dean Watson of St. Marks Church of Seattle and S.R. Gray, a landscape painter from Detroit who was taking Holy Orders. Their business was to organize an Episcopal church on Orcas Island of which Gray was to be the Rector.

They came to me, they said, because I was supposed to be the leading man on the island as they wanted me to help them, etc. I listened to their taffy and told them there must be some mistake, for not only did I not claim to be a leading man, I did not belong to their church and could not subscribe to their doctrines. They said that it made no difference, that their church was very liberal on all questions of personal opinion, that I was a man of good moral standing and one who was very anxious to bring in decent families, that I knew that a church established would be the best of all drawing cards. I admitted this readily and they stayed with us that night. The outcome was that I became their church treasurer and a member of the vestry and subscribed $25 toward building the church and $25 per year towards Mr. Gray's stipend, or salary, which I afterward increased to $35 on condition that Gray should give my children lessons in Latin, etc.

As I had much to do with Mr. Gray in after life, I wish to say a few words here as to what manner of man he was. S.R.S. Gray was a young Englishman of good family and fairly well educated, who lived by his wits in many lands. He was an extremely likeable and gentlemanly fellow who could talk a bird off a bush. He was a keen businessman, but one who in financial matters was absolutely unscrupulous who evidently took up the church calling as an easy and secure living, for he certainly did not believe what he preached. His great mistake was in not becoming a real estate agent.

The church, when built (in 1885) was duly consecrated as Emmanuel Episcopal Church and aided considerably in bringing families. But I was continually in hot water, for Gray

43

would not account to me for collections made if he could possibly avoid it. His recklessness and extravagance would have swamped us if I had not constantly opposed him. He took my opposition always in good part, but his wife fairly detested me. As I had much to do with him, I'll leave him for the present.

7.

As I have already said, our method of combatting the pesty deer was of four kinds. Still hunting, hunting with a fire jack, setting guns and setting stakes. The latter method was probably the most effective and consisted of cutting stakes from young fir trees through which the fire had run the previous year and which were very tough. We sharpened one end and charred it so it could not be seen. Then, choosing a place where the deer had jumped over the fence, we stuck the stake firmly in the ground at the proper angle and the deer were impaled on it. The great danger lay in the fact that these places where the deer jumped over would be the very places where people would cross also. Our guns were set so that the deer in walking would press against a string which was fastened to the trigger.

We certainly got one good scare from this plan. The deer had been destroying my trees and crops very badly and as it was sunset your Mother and I started home but we had not gone a hundred yards when the gun went off and as we had heard Mike Adams' dog barking behind our place and knew that he was there hunting and we knew also that the habit of the deer was never to come into the fields till it was dark, we were in mortal fear that we had shot Adams. So I ran back with my heart in my mouth and was greatly relieved to find a fine large buck there. But it cured me of setting guns though it was almost a universal custom.

Our fire hunting consisted of carrying over the left shoulder an iron basket fitted to a long handle and filled with pitchwood. This not only dazzled the deer and permitted us to approach within easy range, but it made their eyes shine with a greenish glare and made it easy to see them. One of my neighbors killed five one night in one of my fields in a few minutes. Another neighbor killed four in an adjoining field.

The other method was far more laborious and was "still hunting". This necessitated climbing these mountains and crawling through the thickets and the fern and waiting patiently along the deer trails in the dusk. Then we did not dare to move a hand to brush off the pestiferous mosquitoes no matter how badly we were bitten.

The young folks took great pleasure in hunting on the mountain and our boys and their friends from Friday Harbor had many successful hunts. As we could see them coming down the mountainside a mile away we always knew long before they arrived just what luck they had had. Then what appetites they brought with them and what yarns of the big buck that got away, or else they couldn't get close enough for a good shot. At one time they piled nine deer at our door, but that was better luck than usual.

I am now writing about things that occurred during our later years on Orcas Island and while speaking of deer and their depredations I wish to cover the subject and be done with it, so to go back to where I left off. . . .

It was about this time that an old lady from Whatcom named Mrs. Durkee bought my south forty acres for $285 and homesteaded some little fractions that lay between it and the Lime-kiln property. She had a daughter who was crippled and she had taken an Irish boy to raise named S.E. King, who some years later married her daughter and who after the daughter's death, married Ella Kepler a school teacher who became one of your Mother's best friends.

The trail used by the old settlers had followed the lines of least resistance and so wound around and through my valley so as to cut it up badly. I thought that as I furnished the right of way and made the road and kept it in repair, that I'd have some say as to where it ran. So I straightened it out and built my fences accordingly. I had some differences with King on the subject and he claimed that I had invited him to emigrate to a "warmer" climate. Anyhow, the road remains to this day just as I put it in. As I hauled shells from the beach I made it the most beautiful one and a half mile stretch of road in the Northwest at that time and it became quite well known.

I built this road so it ran past what was then known as Ghost Rock, an immense white granite boulder which obtained its eerie name from the Ignis Fatuus that was seen so often in this vicinity. This phosphorescent light evidently escaped from some fissure in the rocks and was only seen on still misty nights and mostly in the spring. We have on several occasions watched it from our windows. It would move slowly along near the ground for a time and resemble nothing so much as a lantern being carried by someone. Then, when moved by a gentle current of air, it would dart up a hundred feet or so and move around there.

It was little wonder that the place got its name of Ghost Rock. This so-called Jack-o-lantern or Will-o-the-wisp was quite common in Canada, but was always seen along the near swamps where there was much decaying vegetation. But in this instance it was near the summit of a dry rocky hill and so was most unusual.

The Roche Harbor Lime Company on San Juan Island having introduced Chinese labor in order to cut prices, the Cascade Lumber Company followed suit and imported a lot of them as wood cutters and as usual they began at once to seek locations for market gardening. As no white family would live near them I thought it time to get busy, so I called a meeting at our house and we organized the Orcas Island Anti-Chinese Association for which I drew up a constitution and laws. These were adopted and friends in Whatcom, Tacoma and Olympia sent for copies for a like organization in those places.

So the Anti-Chinese movement of the Northwest began that had a nation-wide influence. For unlike the sandlot hoodlums of San Francisco, we, while remaining law abiding people, declared that self defense compelled us to protect ourselves from an incursion of a race that was alien to us in every thing. And while disseminating vice among our people they were ruining

47

them financially as our cities were suffering from prevailing hard times. And we were supporting by charity scores of these orientals who in turn sent all money earned out of the country.

Our cause was proven just, for in a short time after the Chinese had been sent away from our Sound cities, business began to mend and the former subjects of charity became self-supporting. As to Orcas Island, our movement was absolutely necessary to prevent the more excitable from taking the law into their own hands which would resort to mob violence. The Chinese were so badly frightened that they sprang onto the steamer before she landed, chattering like a band of magpies.

E.P. Newhall, who was chiefly instrumental in getting (the Chinese) in, flew at me in rage when next we met. But as I was one of his best customers he soon cooled down. I told him that if he did not stand with the people he had better follow the Chinese.

We boasted that thunder and lightning on Puget Sound were unknown but it was hardly correct. Though rare, we did have some very violent electrical storms. The peculiarity is that unlike the East, ours occur almost always during the winter months.

We had a large fir tree struck by lightning on our south field about five years after we began farming. It stood over 200 feet high and the electrical current followed the grain of the wood down it in a spiral, ripping off the heavy bark in a strip a foot in width and flinging it for a hundred feet or more. This tree stood about a quarter of a mile from the house, but the flash and crash seemed to be together and we thought that the house had been struck. Afterward I saw a clump of trees south of Langdon where a dozen or more had been struck. Whether this was caused, as some people claimed, by the hill being a body of low grade iron ore, I do not know, but I do know that this was the only place I ever saw more than one tree struck in the same place.

We quite frequently had earthquake tremors and on one occasion we had quite a respectable quake. We were visiting at Mrs. Durkee's and were sitting at the table playing cards. Her daughter had retired to the room above when the stove suddenly began to dance a jig and we were jumped up and down at a great rate.

The girl began screaming that the house was coming down. While the motion seemed vertical to us it swayed the upper story from side to side. Mr. Van Sant's chimney was badly cracked and an immense fir log over 100 feet long lying above a gorge behind my field was cast into the bottom of the gorge while a log lying on the bluff at the Adam's place was cast into the Bay.

Mr. Gray, who lived at the foot of Turtleback Mountain some six miles distant said that there were rumblings and explosions deep under the mountain. In fact, all of those tremors as they call them, seemed to run from Mt. Constitution by the head of the Bay to Mt. Turtleback and were felt only slightly on the other parts of the island. These two mountains also show traces of volcanic action. Small quantities of lava scoria and pumice are found in their vicinity.

While I was carrying the mail to Doe Bay I saw a shower of frogs, or to be more exact, I came to the spot immediately after they had fallen. I had often heard of this phenomenon as well as showers of fish, both of which taken up by water spouts are sometimes carried far inland. On this day I was caught in a violent summer shower as I followed the trail along Cascade Lake and came suddenly on a space of about 100 yards in extent that literally was a moving mass of little green frogs about 1-1/2 inches in length. They were absolutely countless and simply covered the ground. While not one of the kind were to be seen elsewhere and under no other circumstances could it be explained.

8.

I went to Lopez Island and bought a mare with foal and while she was of good stock I soon found that she was very balky and when the colt grew up he showed the same trait. For though he was a very beautiful animal, he was unmanageable.

When George Sutherland, who was a very conceited fellow offered to trade his little old mare and $15 for him I let him go. George did some tall bragging on how he had bested me in a trade. He said he'd soon cure him of balking, that it was all in knowing how, etc. In fact, to have heard him brag one would have thought him Rarey, the famous horse trader. But the horse soon began his old tricks and George, after beating him very cruelly and even cutting him with an ax in one of his fits of rage, sold him to a stranger on the mainland.

Our island had already become quite famous for the quality of our fruits. Not only for our apples, pears, plums and cherries and other Northern fruits, also some of the more tropical fruits.

Captain Beecher, who had for two years been Treasury Inspector at San Francisco, said that he had never eaten finer Moorpark Apricots than those grown by us. Of course, the Moorpark being a very shy bearer in its native home could not be a very regular bearer with us and we got only a full crop about every third year. When they did bear there was no other peach or fruit that could compare with them.

I remember once when a party of gentlemen were camped on our beach and the question of fruits came up and I said that we had to cut our apricots up in order to can them in Mason jars. One gentleman laughed and said "I'd like to see some of those apricots that can't be put in a Mason jar without being cut up."

The James Tulloch family: First row: Glenn and Stuart. Second row: Lorna, Ida, Eva, Isabel, for whom the *James Francis Tulloch Diary* was written, and Norman. Third row: Laura, Mrs. Annie Brown Tulloch and James Francis Tulloch holding grandson, Pierre Tulloch Barnes.

Gordon Keith

The James Francis Tulloch home on Orcas Island as it appears today.

Not liking to be considered a liar I told him that we had canned all the largest size but that we had a bushel or two of the second size and if he could put them in a Mason jar without cutting them he could have them. He said, "I'm with you, stranger, lead on." So we went up to the house and he sure was a surprised man when he saw them and became a good advertising agent for Orcas Island.

Our house being old and not in the location I wanted it, I went to Whatcom and got material for a new one which I proposed to build on a slight eminence that overlooked all our farm. I failed to get the material there but finally got it at Marysville at the mouth of the Nooksack and after a long search I found a Captain of a tug company who furnished me a scow to load it on. He promised to come for me at a given time to tow it to my place.

I hired a man and got the scow loaded and poled out and anchored there. I waited hour after hour while the tide ran out and left me high and dry on the flats and when it came in again it came with a storm and things certainly looked squally for me. But just when my anchor began to drag badly, driving me towards the shore, the tug came and after a hard pull got me out of danger. After a very rough journey we reached home and I hired two carpenters and built the house, which we afterwards enlarged before we sold the place.

The great herds of sheep naturally became a nuisance after the island was surveyed and homesteaded by white families and the old range claims were at once denied. So we called a meeting and raising the necessary funds sent one of our number to Olympia to lay the matter before the legislature. The result was a stock law requiring all sheep to be enclosed and as soon as the law came into effect we proceeded to enforce it.

Amdrew Newhall in purchasing the Captain Smith place from his squaw after Smith was drowned, claimed that it included all the sheep range on the mountain behind me, though he lived several miles distant. I told him that he must take his sheep up at once, but Andrew Newhall, who always was fair and just, claimed that to take them up at once would be a great hardship and in fact, it would be almost impossible as he had no place to put them. This was June so I told him I'd give him until January 1st and that I'd help him by leaving my fences open behind and so catching them for him. But that after January 1st a sheep or a deer would be the same thing.

He asked if I couldn't go a little farther and give him the pelts, which I readily promised to do for I liked him and certainly didn't want his sheep. I helped him all I could and he got most of them up but shortly after January 1st I saw a band of them on my place and shot them and altogether I killed a score. But some of my neighbors, who had made no such an arrangement, began killing them and when Newhall went after them they told him that I had told them to, which I informed Newhall was a lie. The chief sinner was a fellow named Hughes who rented the Adam's place and was too pious to whistle on Sunday. Andrew Newhall and I always got along well but I did not like his brother S.P. so well. He was as hard as nails.

There was a custom among the squaw men who had sheep in the early days of cutting off the tails of all lambs at round up time each spring. Anyone who had sheep on the range had the right to kill any longtailed sheep at any time. So Charlie Basford, a neighbor of ours who had bought a half dozen weathers and turned them loose boasted that he lived off the increase. I don't believe he overstated his case judging by the number of sheepskins I have seen on the mountainside from time to time. We were very glad when the vexing sheep problem was settled and every man had his just allotment of sheep.

While I was carrying the mail I naturally got very well acquainted with the people along the route as I not only distributed their mail for them but I did a great deal of their trading for them also. So as they considered me something of an expert in grafting and nursery work I had practically all of their work of that kind to do. This made it necessary for me to save a large quantity of scions of all kinds and make up a large amount of grafting wax. Altogether I found it quite profitable, especially as it did not take me from home but a few days at a time.

But the year after I quit carrying the mail Jack Hand came to me and told me I must prepare a graft for the orchard at Metsalady, owned by Peter Jeroup. I told him I could not do it as it would take me away from home too long. But he insisted that I had to, saying he had promised Jeroup that I would. So to get rid of him I said I would go, but not unless I was paid $3.50 per day from the time I left home until I returned and all expenses paid and pay for all material used. I thought this would end it for sure as wages were $1 a day, but he said that was all right, that money was no object when Peter Jeroup wanted anything done. So I had to go. When I arrived I found an old seedling orchard of some 200 trees with their tops so intertwined that I had to cut the tops from several before I could get them on the ground.

It certainly was a mess and while cutting the limbs off and having my helper drag them away an old Yankee Sea Captain whose vessel was loading lumber there entered an earnest protest against my work and declared that I would certainly kill the trees. That it stood to reason that little twigs stuck into the limbs would never grow. That it was clear against nature and that it hurt him to see it done for he'd eaten many an apple off those trees, etc. I asked him what he'd think of me if I came and criticized his manner of loading his boat. He saw the point and went away shaking his head.

This Peter Jeroup evidently belonged to the Dutch nobility and the Danes in his employment, and he would have no others, looked up to him as a superior being. It was not a slavish truckling, but real affection. They seemed to look to him almost as children to a Father, while he in turn treated them as though they were his children. In short, it was a little of the old world transplanted bodily to the new. I was much interested in observing its workings for this almost patriarchal condition was something new to me.

About the middle of the forenoon of the first day the whole crowd of his employees, of which there were perhaps fifty at various occupations, began running toward the hotel, my helper among them. They kept calling something I could not understand and pointing to the hotel. I thought perhaps the hotel was on fire, so I kept on with my work. When my helper came back I asked him what it was all about and found that it was just beer time. That twice a day all hands had free beer. I told him that the next time he ran off without my leave I'd see if Jeroup couldn't give me a man who could tend to business. It almost broke his heart to miss his beer but he had an easy job and knew I'd report him and get another man.

When my scions began to push through, for it was late and they started quickly, it was a never ending marvel to the old Captain and Jeroup and his wife who spent a portion of each day watching the transformation. On my last day Jeroup kept a man with a carriage idle for hours so I would not have to walk the quarter of a mile to the steamer.

While I was there Jeroup showed me the bullet holes in the hotel floor where Tom Robinson, while on one of his drunken sprees, made the Chinese cook dance by firing between his toes. This Tom Robinson lived at the time I carried the mail to Doe Bay, near Olga. Some years later he murdered Jack Hand and was sent to State prison for a number of years.

Robinson was a quiet fellow when sober but a perfect fiend when drunk. I did a quantity of grafting for him at times and got along well with him.

On my return after three weeks absence I found all of my family down with the measles and my orchard nearly ruined by the millions of tent caterpillars that had hatched out in my absence and were stripping every leaf from the trees. As fast as I could knock them off the pests would crawl back up the trunks. As my children took so much of my time and care I was fairly desperate as to how to save my orchard. After all our years of care it was certainly a vital question.

At last I hit on coal tar as the one sticky substance that would not harden but as the coal tar would injure my tender barked young trees I had to put something under the coal tar that would not penetrate through. So I mixed a paste of flour and soft soap and with a swab I made a ring around each trunk. This hardened quickly and I knew that the next winter's rain would loosen it so I then put a ring of tar over it and knocked the pests off once and then once more and it was good to see them gather in great colonies on the trunks, but they could not pass the tar so I saved my orchard. When old Cadwell came from Deer Harbor sometime afterward to see my orchard which he had been informed was in ruins, but which with its new growth was looking fine, he wanted me to come over and ruin his orchard too.

There being no passable roads around the Bay to Eastsound and to take my apples there in a rowboat being a tedious job, we built a crib wharf filled with rock on the south side of the harbor. This was a long, laborious job for your mother and me for she had to hold the boat in place while I built up the logs and rocks. As we could only work when the tide was favorable it was necessarily slow work and very wearying.

While we were building it the children, Ross, Glenn, Eva and Ida were playing along the shore. When Glenn, who was always an active venturesome boy climbed up a high rock to fish and fell into the deep water, your Mother saw it and screamed. I untied the boat as rapidly as I could, our crib where we were

Eastsound in the early 1900's. The dock in the foreground was known as Templin's dock, while the dock in the background was known as Harrison's dock (Standard Oil dock at Madrona Point).

A later photo of Templin and Harrison docks in Eastsound with a view of Jap Island. Note that the Templin dock no longer has the shed on it and a large section of the pilings has given way.

working was some distance from the shore, and pulled as fast as I could but it seemed to go so slowly that I dropped the oars and sprang in and swam. Consequently I was longer in getting there. I got him out and we kept close eyes on the little rascal afterward.

This wharf was better than none, but as my proposed roadway along the bank did not prove feasible I some years later made a large scow which I anchored in deep water with a wire cable attached to a large boulder through which I drilled a hole. But this rock was so massive that I had great difficulty in placing it. The depth at which it lay, the steamers pulled it around as if it were a pebble.

Tiring of such boy's work I went to Whatcom and chartered a piledriving outfit to come and drive me a good pile wharf. The logs for which I had hauled down the mountainside and boomed in the harbor. After the piles were all driven including a runway to the shore, we had a very heavy job of getting the logs on for caps and stringers. But when it was finished we had a track laid to the shore with a car which carried 50 boxes of apples at a load and which could be transferred from the wagon to the wharf in a few minutes. We had the best little dock in the island and one that was a favorite with the Captains.

As I always had a box of apples for the men when shipping I had very little poaching of my cargo. This always was a great cause of complaint. While speaking about my apple shipments which really extended over some thirty-five years and amounted in all to about 75,000 boxes I wish to note a few of my experiences as a shipper.

My chief market for apples was Seattle, but I shipped a good deal to Bellingham, Victoria, Port Townsend and Tacoma and I always accompanied my shipments when possible. I did not like consigning them to commission men. I did fairly well on Western Avenue in Seattle for a number of years by sawing off one commission man against another, but finally they combined and the price to be paid was daily agreed upon. Then began the plunder game that gradually ruined fruit growing on the island.

Among my earlier experiences I remember taking 750 boxes of 20-ounce apples which I succeeded in selling to a Western Avenue man at a good price, but when it came to paying for them he put me off with excuses until after banking hours. He then told me to go home and bring another cargo that I had promised him and he would settle for both. I consented provided he gave me an endorsement by some good Seattle firm that I knew. This he refused to do, claiming that he would not be under obligation to any of them. So we began to wrangle for an hour or two for I knew he wanted the apples and I was determined that he would not have them without paying for them. Finally he took me to a North Seattle stylish bawdy house where he seemed to be very much at home and got the money from the madam and paid me. When I got back with my next shipment he had skipped the country owing everybody.

These fellows pay a month's rent in advance and hang out their signs and are ready to fleece the unwary farmer and fruit growers out of thousands of dollars. This whole commission business is a disgrace to our state and is little short of highway robbery.

At another time I took a shipment to Port Townsend and also to Portland, Oregon. We could not agree on terms though I saw he wanted my apples and while I stood in a deep doorway puzzling as to what I had better do I overheard Pettygrove and his partner putting up a job to get my apples for a song.

They said, "Just wait till the steamer Premier, 'which was on her weekly trip to Vancouver,' is gone and he'll have to take whatever we offer him or keep them here for a week and pay wharfage and have them ruined by the rats."

As they were the only large buyers in that place I waited till they had gone and hurried to the custom house and took out my manifest for Vancouver. Pettygrove, who had been on the watch met me at the bottom of the stairs and wanted to know what I was doing there. I told him I was taking out my manifest for Vancouver. As the Premier was in sight the change in his tone was laughable. We came to terms at once. The only stipulation being that I should take my season's supplies out in

59

trade, which I agreed to in writing, provided he could furnish me with what I wanted and as cheaply as anyone else. So I went to Waterman and Katy who, thinking that mine would be a cash sale, gave me very fair prices. When I went to Pettygrove with this price list he fairly made the air blue and never quite forgave me for holding my own.

One of my most amusing experiences was with my first shipment to Victoria. I was a total stranger and on paying duty on my cargo I learned that there were only two men there who handled cargoes of that size. One was an old Scotchman who I had often heard of on our island and the other a man who, knowing that I had already been to see the Scotchman, whom I found to be loaded with apples, offered me a ruinous price and I found on investigating that no one could sell without a license which was so high that I could not afford it for one cargo. So I did a very cheeky thing. I went to the old Scotchman and showing him just what I was up against, asked him to let me sell my shipment on his license as his agent. He looked me up and down and said:

"You didn't leave any of your gall at home did you? Don't you know that you are asking me to authorize you to sell your apples to my customers in my name while I am loaded with apples which I am trying to sell?"

I acknowledged that he was correct, but the outcome was that he gave what I asked for and wouldn't take pay for it. He said that he guessed that I could travel on my nerve.

I shipped to him a number of times after that on consignment for I had absolute confidence in him, and when he died some years later I felt I had lost a good friend.

My annual shipments during later years on the farm were from 3000 to 4000 boxes, which, added to the products from 120 cherry trees and 325 prune trees, a score of pear and plum trees and from two to three acres in strawberries, made ours a very busy life indeed. During the later years the insect and fungus pests became so bad that spraying the trees became an expensive and laborious affair, as we had about 1700 trees of all kinds.

One attempt to swindle me out of a fine shipment of apples was made by Bander and Pace, merchants at Eastsound who were in a shaky condition financially and with whom I agreed as to price, but they said they wanted to just run over to Vancouver with them and bring me the money back. I stayed with them till midnight trying to get the money from them and refusing to give them the apples without (payment). We parted on none too good terms and I was not surprised the next day to learn they had skipped the country. Having turned their little stock of goods over to another man named Rudolph and with whom they had been doing business for several days previous.

I had bought quite a bill of goods from them during this time, paying cash and taking receipt. I was not a little surprised when sometime later Rudolph presented me with a bill for the same and demanded payment. He scoffed at me when I told him I had a receipt for it, but when I brought it to him he declared that he never authorized them to receipt for money paid and that I must pay him. I told him to "tell it to the Marines" that a firm was always responsible for receipts given by their clerks and that I only paid my debts once. When he found he couldn't bluff me and I was not going to be moved the old rogue actually cried. He said that Bander and Pace had fleeced him shamefully and that he was a poor man with a family, etc. I foolishly paid him half the amount again and told him that I would share the loss with him, but I'm certain they were all a gang of rascals.

This George Bander was a son-in-law of my neighbor, whose daughter believed him to be quite wealthy as he had hired a carriage from Seattle and boasted of having $20,000 and although he cut quite a figure. He made such a wide swath and so dazzled the poor girl's eyes that she thought him a regular Prince Charming. While all the fellow had was unlimited gall and two children by his first wife. But that's an old game in marital affairs. They say "all's fair in love and war" but what a dispeller of illusions the honeymoon must be.

9.

When the trial of George Phillip's squaw came on at Port Townsend I had a good deal of idle time on my hands so I walked around the docks and the beaches a good deal. Jimmie Guthrie, who was also there asked me one day to go with him to the Duke of York's camp. The Indian who carried this high sounding name was camped with his band on the beach near town. So I went to see the Duke in his castle. Said castle being really something. It was about 100 feet long by 12 feet wide and consisted of stakes driven into the ground with cross pieces tied to them in any old way and pieces of old sails and skins of various animals laid on them with sufficient holes left at the top to let out a portion of the smoke caused from several fires of beachwood which were all down the center.

We had arrived at meal time and a score or more were gathered around a large kettle in which was a hash of boiled fish, mainly halibut. Table manners consisted of reaching in with their hands and grabbing chunks of what they fancied and stowing it away where it would do the most good. I watched the performance for a time comparing them with the proud fierce Indians of the plains. Guthrie asked them in Chinook if they knew his squaw? They all shook their heads and said "Halo no", but finally one old squaw cried out, "Nawkitka, yes. Yamouth, Yamouth" and Guthrie turned to me and said with pride, "You see, I can find relations wherever I go."

Another trip I made to Port Townsend which I certainly will never forget was when Mr. Setzer, "Col." May and I were summoned on the jury and to go on the weekly steamer would keep us there for several days before the court convened so we arranged to have Ned Barnes take us in his little 2-1/2 ton plunger. But May backed out and went by steamer declaring that good men were too scarce for such risks in March.

We sailed through Thatcher Pass and struck a bad riptide and our center board jammed and we had a close call. When we at last got clear and out of the Pass we struck such a gale that we were glad to run in behind a little island on the south side of Decatur Island. This is only an island at low tide I believe. We lay there for two days and when the storm subsided somewhat we started again for our destination. Late on a stormy March evening we rounded Point Partridge only to be met by a head wind and head tide which was beginning to run out strong. We tacked back and forth across the channel and once again came within a little of being able to pass Point Wilson. The tide was now running very strong, adding to the gale made us begin to lose ground, but we kept struggling hour after hour losing ground at every tack. At one time we came within an ace of being run down in the darkness by a large lumberman which fairly scraped our vessel.

At last Barnes gave up, turned and ran for Point Partridge there to drop anchor and lie until morning, or until the tide turned. Just as we were rounding the point a squall from over Whidbey Island threw our boat over on her side and it sure did look like it was all day for us. Mr. Setzer was down below and hopelessly seasick. The false ballast had broken loose and piled on one side thus preventing the old tub from righting herself, but worst of all the stove had fallen over with the danger of setting us afire.

Barnes yelled to me to right the stove and to try and shift the rock ballast back while he crawled out and dragged the sail out of the water. Maybe I didn't have a merry time of it. I burned my hands on the red hot stove, but finally managed to get things moved around so that with Barnes getting the sail dragged in she righted herself without taking in much water. We anchored there, tumbling around until morning.

While we were upset and fighting for our lives I kept my eyes on the hatch covers as the only thing that would help me to keep afloat. Though with both wind and tide driving down the straits we would have been absolutely helpless. We sailed up to Port Townsend the next day and there was old "Col." May strutting around on the dock. When we landed he said in his pompous style "It's all right, Mr. Tulloch, I've explained it all to the judge and you won't be fined." This was a little more than I could stand so I replied "You go to hell. I will do my own explaining."

After the island settled up the people began to demand persistently that I should build a sawmill on my stream for the benefit of the island as all the lumber had to be brought at great expense from Whatcom or Port Townsend. They even accused me of playing dog in the manger and talked as though my stream was public property and demanding that I either build on it or lease it to someone who would.

Amos Hill, who with his sons had been in the business and who had long looked hungrily at my place offered to loan the amount of money necessary to start the mill at 12-1/2% interest and take a mortgage on my place for security. But singular as it may seem I was not greatly impressed by the charitable offer. Calling the people together I made them this proposition.

I have the stream I told them, with power enough to run a little sawmill and it will take me $1500 to establish it. I'll have to mortgage my place to raise the amount. I know nothing of the business and the chances are ten to one that I'll fail and lose everything. As to your other proposition that I should lease to someone who could bring in a lot of undesirable people and locate them in front of my home I'll not listen to for a moment. Now as to your first proposal, if you will jointly secure me with some legal liens on your homes, that you will keep me continually supplied with logs, taking your pay in lumber, for that was your proposal, I'll go into it. But unless you do secure me I'll have nothing to do with it. This they refused to do and left me and went to John Carle who had a place 1-1/2 miles from tidewater on a stream from the mountain lake. He had a fine body of timberland and they succeeded in their efforts with him where they had failed with me. With the natural results that in a year or two he lost his home and was laughed at for his gullibility.

Shortly before this, while working in our garden, we saw a fine vessel of some 300 tons drop anchor in the middle of the Bay in front of our place and shortly after a boat left her manned by a dozen sailors and pulled onto our beach. The one in command introduced himself to us as Captain Forney of the U.S. Geodetic and Coast Survey. He said that his present business was to triangulate the straits. He wanted to know if I could guide him to the top of Mt. Constitution. I saw a chance to make a dollar and told him I could. He told me to be ready the next morning at 8 a.m.

After he left your mother said "Now you've done it, you were never there in your life." I said that's true enough but it would be hard if an old mountain man can't find the mountain top. I'll have to try at it anyway as Uncle Sam is a good paymaster.

That night I laid my plan to follow the county trail along Cascade Lake to the south end of the mountain which was quite bare of timber, and by climbing it there and keeping well ahead of Captain Forney so as to escape embarrassing questions. I thought that once on top of Mt. Constitution I'd be able to locate the highest peak without exposing my ignorance.

When Forney came in the morning he wore high riding boots which I knew would make climbing very difficult for him. After we left the trail and began our steep ascent he kept calling out every little while, "Pass word along for the guide to halt." But as our party was composed of about a score and were strung along down the mountainside I only halted until a party of them arrived, when I would go on again. Always keeping in advance I at last arrived at the top of the mountain and saw near me a bare peak which seemed to be the highest point so I headed for it and when Captain Forney arrived and had somewhat recovered from his climb he looked around and said: "Is this the highest point?" I did not like the tone of his voice and so to hedge I said, "Why, yes, I think it's higher than the other one." I did not know there was another one. He said, "Can you take me to the other one?" I said, "Sure, I'll climb this tree and set a straight course for it." This I did and saw another peak away up at the northwest part of the mountain which was the only other high point in sight.

It was nearly two miles away and a deep, heavily timbered gorge lay between. So we started and as before I kept out of his way until I had reached the bottom of the gorge where the creek from the marsh flows toward the big lake. When Captain Forney overtook me he was badly out of humor and declared that I had been lost, that I was going down the mountain instead of up. I told him he'd soon get all the climbing he wanted and that we were making a beeline for the other peak.

After much climbing and many halts, for the Captain was all in, we reached the peak and Forney showed me how he knew the other peak was not the right one. He had an official record of an ascent made a score of years ago by the British who had piled a large cairn of rock and hoisted a balloon, the hoop of which was still there. We proceeded to hunt for the flagpoles which we got near the swamp below and then found that he had forgotten the flag. Forney and several men tore up their jumpers and made a flag and hoisted it.

Captain Forney asked me to take him back the shortest way possible so we struck out southwest skirting the marshes and shortly before coming to the rim of Mt. Constitution we came to a beautiful little marsh of about an acre, set like a jewel in the timber and on to the north side of it there boiled up out of the solid rock a little spring of the purest water and icy cold. Captain Forney was enchanted with it for we both recognized it as an artesian, as there was no higher land from which it could have come. So perforce it came under the sea from the Cascade Range. Forney said this will be your camping place for I want you to grade me a good pack trail to the summit and clear away all the timber there that can obstruct the view. Which I did that summer. This trail was long known as the Government Trail and was used much by the tourists until the wagon road was built nearer the Mountain Lake.

Some years later a big hulking fellow named James Fry whose girl had thrown him over christened this beautiful little spring

"Bleeding Heart Spring", a name I fear it will always carry.

When we got back Captain Forney insisted that I should go on board his vessel and take supper with him as he had some instructions to give me. While I was looking over his splendid library while waiting for supper I overhead Captain Forney saying to his sailing master, "I'll bet five dollars our guide was never up on Mt. Constitution before." So I didn't fool him after all.

The Captain bought all of his vegetables from us that summer and when Mike Adams tried to undersell us and take the trade away he got royally snubbed. We were all very sorry when Captain Forney's uncle, the owner of Forney's Press of Philadelphia, died and made him his heir and he went east.

One of the most beautiful sights I ever witnessed, but one that must be quite common to our airmen, was while I was cutting down the timber on the peak which obstructed the view of the triangulation points, one of which was Mt. Dallas on San Juan Island, the other was in the Gulf of Georgia.

While working there one day the whole lower Sound country became enveloped in a dense fog which completely shut from view the whole of the Island Archipelago, with the exception of the little mass of rock on which I stood of about 100 feet in extent and which seemed to be a solitary islet in an illimitable sea. Except that far to the east Mt. Baker and a few of the snowy peaks broke through, but the great billowy mass, fleecy white in the sunshine, seemed never still for a moment, but weaved and wound in the most peculiar and fascinating manner and utterly unlike the clouds seen from below; which may look drab and dark grey or golden, but these were always fleecy white and beautiful. What glorious views our birdmen must have when riding far above the clouds.

I remember well an experience I had while prospecting on the summit of the Divide between James Creek and Lefthand Creek in Colorado. I had sunk my prospect shaft the ten feet required before recording and had gone back that day to finish things up to leave for the season. While working up there I could hear thunder rumbling far below, though the sun shone brightly where I was. Having finished my work I gathered my tools and with the heavy load of steel consisting of pick, bar, hammer, drill gads, etc., I started down the mountainside when shortly before entering the cloud strata and just where my trail led along a precipice I was dazzled and partly stunned by a flash and crash and I instinctively flung the load of steel I was carrying over the precipice. When I got down to the camp on James Creek I found it almost washed out by the torrential rains that had deluged them while I had been working in the sunshine.

10.

Among those who came to make their home on Orcas Island was a man named John Swerdfiger, a printer on the Anacortes newspaper, who homesteaded a claim along the north shore of Cascade Lake and who made his home there. He lived with us while making some improvements on his place.

John became a great friend of us all, but especially of the children to whom he was always kind and considerate. He was very studious and being somewhat of a dreamer had become thoroughly embued with the beauty of theoretical Socialism and really believed that a system which is theoretically the perfection of government could be adopted by imperfect human beings who show themselves so poorly fitted to exercise even the representative form we are trying to make a success.

After several years spent on Orcas Island John Swerdfiger went to Pasadena and from there to Washington, D.C. where he became infatuated with the occult nonsense of Annie Besant and the other Theosophists. He died before his time through an attempt to follow out some of her Theosophical tomfoolery. We were deeply grieved to see John take up this miserable rubbish of Eastern fakers for he was really a very able man and one of the best, though impractical. His brother, Dan, took up the adjoining claim along the lake but did not keep it long.

It was about this time that the people made me the Justice of the Peace and during the time I held office I married a Mr. John Mattison and a daughter of a neighbor, Mr. Van Sant, also a Mr. Walter Still and Miss Sarah Dixon. I also tried one man from Waldron Island for sheep stealing, but my chief duties were drawing up of legal instruments. One which had an important after result was an agreement that I drew between M.L. Adams and his wife, the daughter of J.N. Fry of Eastsound, by which he paid her $300 for her relinquishment of all claims for community property rights. As some years after Adams sold his place to Baxter and Peters of Seattle for about $8000 and the former Mrs. Adams who had become something of a notorious character, filed a claim on Baxter and Peters for her share of the property and they were worried greatly about this cloud on the title. But when I heard of it and informed Baxter he hurried to our recorder's office and got a copy of the agreement and showed it to her lawyer who was furious. Judge Green was Baxter's attorney and he complimented me on the careful manner in which it was drawn and said that he could not have done it better himself. It is hardly necessary to add that this did not make me more of a favorite of Fry.

During my term in office I was called up from bed one night by George McGonagle, the Superintendent of the Lime Works, who said that W.D. Scott, the firm that ran it, had failed completely and as they had not paid their men for several months and winter was coming on they were in a bad way. He wanted my advice as to what to do. I told him to call the men together and explain matters to them and tell them that each would have the right to anything in the store at cost price, up to the amount due them as long as the goods lasted.

He agreed and such a scramble I have never seen. Each man had his pile on the ground, some things were useful, but a great deal of the stuff was absolutely of no value to them. McGonagle refused to take anything and never got a cent. He was a man in every sense of the word. He afterward went to Seattle and by natural ability became Chief of the City Field Engineer force. One young fellow whose Mother, a widow, depended on him for support could not use the store goods and was all broken up over it. So as I owed the company some money for supplies I went to Mr. McGonagle and had him transfer the account, much to the pleasure of the young man whom I paid soon after.

The early settlers having used Arbutus Point (now Madrona Point) at Eastsound as a burying ground we thought it a good move to secure title to it from the government. As situated as it was it was likely to be filed on by some schemer and trouble ensue. I was made Chairman of the Board of three, the others being M.L. Adams and J.N. Fry, and ordered to acquire title if possible in the name of Orcas Island Cemetery Association. The two others as usual turned the matter over to me to attend to. I corresponded with government officials and found that they could not deed the land to the association, but that we could acquire title in our joint names and then deed it to the association. This we proceeded to do and having acquired title in our joint names I wanted to turn it over at once. But S.R.S. Gray and some of the others put up a job to sell the point and purchase a cemetery site further back and remove the dead to it. This I opposed, both because so many of the dead could not be located and because I knew it would make no end of trouble. Most of the Indians and half-breeds were Catholic and they comprised nine tenths of all who were buried there.

The new cemetery would be considered as Protestant, or non-sectarian at least. I wanted to avoid trouble that was sure to follow. So as Chairman of the Board of Trustees I called a meeting of the people to vote on it and in the meantime I went to Seattle on business. As luck would have it our mail steamer broke down and the passengers were tied there so that we did not arrive until the day after the meeting was to be held.

I feared for the results for Gray and Harrison wanted to buy it. I knew they were very anxious to carry their scheme through and might take advantage of my absence. When I stepped off the boat Rev. Gray came up smiling and informed me that it was all right that they had held the meeting and voted unanimously for the transfer and all I had to do was to sign the deed as Adams and Fry had already done so.

I learned afterward what they got for doing it. I asked how many of the old settlers and Indians and half-breeds were present and voted and he said they did not come at all. I said "why didn't you postpone the meeting when you knew I couldn't get there?" Eb Harrison who with his brother, were the purchasers and who, with Rev. Gray had put up the job, interfered here and insolently ordered me to sign the deed or take the consequences. This I refused to do until I had time to look further into it. I told them plainly that they had acted in an underhanded manner and that I doubted if I should sign it at all.

They were furious when they found they could not intimidate me. Gray then induced them to fall back on the old arbitration dodge to make my friends believe that I was simply obstinate if I refused to arbitrate. As I already believed that they had the law on their side as I had given the half-breeds due notice and their failure to attend and vote clearly deprived them of any legal right to object. I consented and chose Amos Hill whom I knew to be honest, though easily influenced. They chose of course, one of their gang and easily induced Mr. Hill to agree to a friend of theirs named Guye for the third. It was of course settled before it began and I was ordered to sign the deed which I did.

It was no sooner done than the half-breeds, who would not attend when duly notified, got busy and hired a lawyer and brought suit, claiming very large damages and making me chief defendant, though they knew that I alone had been fighting their battle for them. They cooly explained it by saying it was damages they were after and that I was their best bet. But the fact was that the half-breed element had always held a grudge against me because they knew I was opposed to miscegenation and had worked hard to get in the white families.

Fry, Adams and the Harrisons hired a Seattle lawyer and brought him to me to prepare their case, or our case, as they called it, but I positively refused to have anything to do with them and they left in a rage. When the case came to trial before Judge Winn at Friday Harbor and the Judge asked the defense who appeared for them they named their attorney. I told the Judge that I had nothing to do with him (attorney). That while I knew the saying that the man who is his own lawyer has a fool for a client. Still, as I had come there to state the facts in the case and had opposed the transfer I would employ no council.

My position seemed to please the Judge who often referred to me regarding the disputed points and treated me with real courtesy. The people hadn't a ghost of a chance from the first, having been duly notified by me, they had failed to attend and exercise their rights to vote and so lost the case. When it was over the lawyer hired by Fry and Adams sent me a bill at once. I told him to kindly let me know when he got it. And so ended the graveyard case, as it was called.

I found that much of my orchard was either an inferior quality of fruit or unsuited to this climate so I was compelled to graft over a great portion of it which meant another long wait for a yield of fruit. But as we were the pioneers in the business we had to do the experiment.

Not being able to get a satisfactory price for my hay on the Island in one of the years before my orchard came into bearing, I chartered William Fry's schooner and we took it to Seattle. We surely had a very wary trip of it. We rolled around on the straits the first day and night and the next morning we got carried by the tide about halfway to Seattle and anchored there till the tide turned. Then we started again and twenty-four hours later we managed to drop anchor in practically the same place. But the very next day we got through and I did very well with my shipment of hay. But this was quite enough of windjamming for me.

11.

These San Juan Islands are a cluster of mountain peaks composed of metamorphic sandstone that through the heat and pressure almost resemble granite. Having been forced up through the overlying strata tilting it at a sharp angle to the north, this chain of mountain peaks seems to extend from the Mt. Baker region in the Cascade Range to the mountains of Vancouver Island. And throughout they are more or less mineralized.

It is little wonder that the early settlers who were largely from the Cariboo and other western mining camps should have their curiosity aroused by the many mineralized outcroppings on the Island.

The first work done was on Guemes Island where a vein of copper ore carrying a low grade value in gold was opened by a man named O'Brien. But it was soon abandoned through faulting. The excitement having spread to Orcas Island soon became intense and nearly everyone had dreams of sudden wealth for the next year or two.

All conversations seemed interlarded with geological and mineralogical terms while the secrecy and confidences made the island people resemble a lot of Guy Fawks conspirators. In common with the rest I took a hand in this search for the pot of gold at the rainbow's end. For the outcroppings were really promising and in Colorado where I had mined they would easily have procured the necessary capital for their investment. But lying here at our very doors, capital would not look at them. I really believe that some of these prospects would, with depth, make paying mines.

McKay and Warbass of Friday Harbor sank fifty feet on a quartz ledge on the north side of Turtleback Mountain. Although showing only a copper stain at the surface it gave at the bottom a quantity of ore that was all high grade. But having obtained a patent for their claim all work was suspended through lack of means. And it remains so at this time.

I found a quartz outcropping on the same mountain that gave some rainbow copper ore that assayed at $25 a ton. But after blasting some 15 feet in hard white quartz I had to give it up as the cost was too great.

The principal prospecting was along the shore which was a mistake as not only was the assay value less but the rock was shaken and faulted. Higher up the rock seemed fairly firmly in place as in other mining camps I had been in. In fact, the greater part of their so-called discoveries along the shore were barren deposits of sulphuret of iron, but the owners certainly walked on air for a while and considered themselves in the Rockefeller and Vanderbilt class.

There was some very fair ore ground found on the east side of Blakely Island but it was so near the sea level and the rock so seamy that it could not be worked.

When a man named Welsh found a vein of Galena ore on the north side of Mt. Constitution I became really interested and began prospecting our mountain and having found a body of blue-gray quartz that assayed $2 a ton in silver on the surface I went in with David Baxter of the Guarantee Loan & Trust Company of Seattle and we spent a couple of hundred dollars on it. But the value did not increase with depth so we quit it. But our work was superficial and the ledge might have proved a paying proposition if properly developed.

In prospecting higher up on the mountainside I found an out-cropping that interested me and having sunk a shaft about a dozen feet I began to get small quantities of really high grade Argentiferous Galena ore, the ore found by Welsh being simply Galena and carrying little or no silver. But this was high grade silver ore, so I determined on developing it to the full extent of my means. But just at that time a Vermont Yankee named

Tiffany filed a timber claim on the tract. To contest his claim I'd have to prove that I had mines of proven value, which I did not as yet have, so I filled the shaft and left it.

This has always been a sore point with me for if there is a body of such ore below, it would mean a fortune to the owner. I afterward showed a piece of that ore to Tom McGeever, an old Colorado miner, and he declared at once that it came from the famous silver mine there that he had formerly worked in. When I told him that I dug it out of the side of Mt. Constitution he said:

"Tulloch, I've known you for a good time and that is the first time you ever lied to me."

Nor could I make him believe otherwise.

This practically ended my mining on Orcas Island and having lost several hundred dollars at it I looked around to see if I could recoup myself out of the Lime excitement, then beginning. I had while prospecting on Turtleback Mountain, seen a ledge on the west side of Baldnob that I believe was Lime rock though everyone else had passed it by on account of its dark color. I filed on it, much to the amusement of the little Englishman, Ned Hichens, with whom I had been prospecting and who lived in the vicinity. He declared not only was it not lime rock but that it was on patented Richards land. But I had observed that the reddish brown coloring in lime rock was generally due to oxides of minerals and left the lime dark and unsalable. While the black coloring matter being vegetable would burn out and leave the lime white. So I burned some and found it to be excellent.

I then sent to Olympia and got the field notes of that section and fixing my compass with a Jacobs staff I took my two boys, Ross and Glenn, and hunting up a meander stake on the shore as a starting point we scaled the cliff by hanging to the bushes growing there. We ran out lines and found that the ledge was off the Richards land by some forty feet. But there had been some excitement about marble deposits, as some of the lime rock will take a fine polish, though it cracks badly on exposure,

76

certain parties named Oldham and Moody had located the land between me and the beach for what little rock there was in it.

As I had to have an outlet for mine I bought them out for $250. I also bought an eighty acre tract of patented land from Oldham that had some lime rock on it and some very rich marsh land. I now had my claim in shape to sell, but before I could do anything a former land office official from Seattle jumped my claim and filed a stone and timber claim on it. He evidently thought I would contest it. When the case came up for trial and he saw me there with my witnesses, he left. Then after I had gone home he filed a homestead claim on it though it did not have a foot of agricultural land on it.

We had to appear again and though I had beaten him off I was getting tired of it and anxious to sell. I went to Tacoma and sold it to a contractor of $700 which he paid me $300 as a forfeit, the balance to be paid in two months. He failed to make good and asked for more time. I gave him a month more but he gave it up and forfeited the amount paid. So it was on the market again.

Rev. S.R.S. Gray said that he had a friend in Seattle, a member of his church, who he thought might buy it and wanted my best terms. I told him he could have all over $1000 he could get for it. He got a month's time and when that was gone he came for more, saying that things were going well. So I gave him a month more and raised the price to $1200. Rev. Gray got his man to come to Orcas Island and I went with them to see the property.

The gentleman was a prominent member of St. Marks Church of Seattle and from the time we left till we returned Gray never once mentioned Lime rock, except once while we ate lunch at the foot of the ledge he casually remarked, "It's a fine body of rock." His whole conversation was about the Lord Jesus Christ and what he had done for us poor sinners. I never heard a person talk so much shop before. But it was no business of mine.

When the time was up Rev. Gray said that the bargain was practically concluded, but that he was English and they took so much time in going over titles. He wanted 10 days more which I gave him at $1600. He kicked about the raise but went to Seattle to hurry things up. When his ten days were gone he vowed that everything was complete except some legal papers which had to be made out and he wanted more time. I said, "Mr. Gray, you take the boat to Seattle and I'll take the boat tomorrow for Whatcom and if I receive the $1600 by telegraph by 6 p.m. it will be all right, but if not my price will be $2500. By six the next morning I got my money and I signed the deed for $2200 which gave Gray $600 for his work.

Now this was fair, but when the gentleman informed me at a later date that Gray told him that I got the full $2200 and that he was doing it solely for friendship for a brother in Christ I was not much surprised, for I had learned to size him up long before.

I later sold a lime claim to Captain Glover for $280 and took some satisfaction in the trade. R.A. Ballinger who was afterward Secretary of the Interior was Glover's attorney and he did all he could to prevent the deal. But this money did me little good as like everyone else at the time I caught the real estate craze that swept the Sound country and blew it for a lot in Port Townsend. I also gave $500 and the land I bought from Oldham for three lots in Anacortes which I still hold. But I doubt very much if I'll ever get my money back for them. I also got a lot in Des Moines and Gray Hambly and I jointly bought two lots in Fidalgo City, which are practically worthless. I have no apology to offer for these bad deals except that the craze seemed to sweep everyone off their balance and I was no more sensible than the rest.

I have lost the only good opportunity that I had to invest through the lack of enterprise of one member of our church vestry. During one of my trips to Seattle I had made arrangements by which we could obtain some twenty acres at the edge of what is now becoming the wholesale district, on the installment plan and at such reasonable rates that the members of our vestry without hardship could have made the monthly payments. On my return I laid the offer before them. Rev. Gray was keen for it and Hambly, who always followed Gray's lead, agreed. The others would have come in but Eph Langell who is best described as a "cultus" drawled out, "No by gool, I'd rather spend my money for good whiskey." That threw cold water on the whole proposition. Had we secured this property it would have made us all fairly wealthy.

12.

It is almost impossible now to realize the rivalry that then existed between the Sound cities, each of which claimed to be the coming metropolis of the Sound, each struggling to build themselves up and discrediting the others.

I remember one incident of this which I watched in Anacortes. The tide in Guemes Channel, which is the Anacortes waterfront, runs about six miles an hour and so vessels are anxious to make a landing at once. A little sternwheeler from Seattle lay in the middle of the ocean dock leisurely unloading when they saw a large ocean liner from Frisco coming up the channel. The wharfinger tried to get them to either hurry up or move along to make room for the big vessel which lay waiting to dock. This they positively refused to do and ceased their unloading.

Finally, the wharfinger who had tried time after time to cast off their lines lost his patience and seized an ax and was going to cut their hawser loose when the captain sprang from the pilot house with a club and knocked the wharfinger down. Then casting off going to Whatcom. On their return an officer went aboard with a warrant for the captain's arrest but they pulled loose and carried the officer to Seattle.

This was called good business. But it was just such cutthroat business tactics combined with a pull together policy that has made Seattle the Queen City of the Sound. For business is war and war is just what Sherman called it.

Dr. Nevins made us a second visit about this time and Rev. Gray got up a church picnic to be held at Sucia Island. Dr. Nevins who was a naturalist wished to investigate the fossils that were so abundant there in that sandstone group. As I was a member of the vestry and treasurer of the church must needs go as there was church business to be tended to. I took Ross and Glenn along and we spent a very pleasant day and the Doctor who had his powerful microscope with him took great pleasure in opening up to the boys the world of the infinitely small. He showed them the countless forms of life on all sea grasses and plants which will be a day they will long remember.

While prospecting on Turtleback Mountain I ran across the anchor of which I had heard the old settlers speak of so often. It was on a bare piece of rock some hundred feet in extent at the very summit of the mountain overlooking Douglas Channel and the Gulf of Georgia and its magnificent group of islands. It consists largely of a number of small rock laid in the form of an immense anchor and a short piece of cable. The first settlers found the rocks of which it is composed just as moss covered and ancient looking as when I saw it, thus showing that it is a record of a visit of long ago. Most probably it was put there by early explorers of these islands who would naturally climb to this mountain peak for the view and being sailors would be apt to leave an anchor as a momento.

I was interested in noting the great number of white granite boulders scattered along the mountainside on the island from sea level up to about 300 feet above. The nearest granite of that character, in place, is in S.E. Alaska and would certainly seem to show that these rocks were carried here by the icebergs in past ages. Which, upon reaching warmer seas and being stranded on these lower hills and mountainsides which were then submerged, left these rocks scattered on what were then banks and reefs. Some of them still rest on the very edge of cliffs thus showing conclusively the manner in which they were deposited. Some idea might be formed of the time at which it occurred by the known slow, but regular rate at which this coast is rising.

I found near where my stream enters my harbor, a bed of flange oyster shells about four feet above high tide. This was where I excavated into the bluff for a roadway. They could not

81

have been put there. While this kind of shellfish is only found in fairly deep water. In excavating for my apple house at about 60 feet above the present high tide I dug into an extensive former clam beach. Exactly like the present one except that the beach mud had hardened into a semi-rock and the lime forming the shells was nearly all gone leaving it a mass of the imprints of clam, oyster, cockle and muscle shells and sea worms along with other inhabitants of the present mud flats. Those I dug out at the mouth of the creek were fairly well preserved.

13.

I found quite a difference between the Flora and Fauna of the island compared with that of the adjacent mainland. In animals we had numerous deer of a species considerably smaller than those of the mainland. Although we had no elk or cariboo they had simply been exterminated by the Indians as we frequently found their horns on the mountainside. The only other animals were the brown mink which infested the waterfront and the raccoon that lived in the forests. An occasional otter following the peculiar habits of that animal crossed our highest mountains on its travels from sea to sea, going up creeks on one side to their source and thence across to the water on the other side.

Of birds we had the ever present gull whose gloomy and discordant cry became terribly monotonous. The fish-eating ducks that swarmed in our water when herring and smelt were in. There were also migratory birds in their season as well as pestiferous crows and jaybirds and an occasional magpie and eagles.

The crows lived chiefly along the beaches, except when the fruit was ripe and then they became a veritable scourge. The jaybirds were the torment of our lives during the early years until I found out how to control them. They were extremely fond of potatoes and scratched them out and carried them off, or pecked them if large enough and destroyed them. But the worst of all was at planting time, for as soon as the seed was dropped in the rows and before it could be covered they dropped down in scores from the trees and levied so heavy a toll that it became unendurable and nearly drove us crazy. For they, like crows, were too cunning to let us approach them with a gun. But at all times they were so brazen in their plundering that nothing that could be devised to destroy them would have seemed wrong.

I tried trapping them with the figure four trap, but they would eat the peas from around it and even under the spindle without springing the trap. Their provoking cry as they flew away almost sounded like malicious laughter. So remembering the plan to drive away rats by singeing one, I determined to catch one of the pests, pluck it naked and let it go with only its wing and tail feathers left.

Having soaked some peas I threaded on a string I tied it to a spindle and caught a male bird, which I plucked absolutely naked except its wings and tail. In spite of its cries and the protestations of your Mother who was very angry with me, and called me some choice names, I got some high colored calico and tearing it in strips I tied long streamers to its legs and let it go. It flew directly into the woods uttering a peculiar shrill cry continuously. This must have been their S.O.S. for the jaybirds came in legions and swarmed into the trees. In fact, they seemed to be holding a jaybird convention and had we understood jaybird language I have no doubt that we would have heard things we would not have liked. At all events they evidently decided to pass a resolution that we Tullochs were not fit company for self-respecting jaybirds to associate with for they suddenly left our neighborhood en masse and we had little trouble with them from that day on.

We had most of the timber found in this latitude, such as douglas fir, hemlock, spruce, cedar, balsam fir, alder, willow, soft maple and madrona. Also a few specimens of oak and wild cherry. Among the shrubs we had flowering current, salmon berry, salal, wild rose, gooseberry, blackcaps, the running blackberry and strawberry. There were also a greater variety of lychen and moss than I have ever seen anywhere else. From the trailing moss that hangs in streamers and festoons from trunks and limbs of trees and almost equals the Spanish moss of the south.

The lychens which cling close to every stone and log thoroughly camouflage this region. Here as well as farther north they make the work of the prospector extremely difficult. We are totally exempt from that pest of the mainland woods, the Devil Club, which is surely well named. This cactus-like shrub which makes travel in these northern forests often a martyrdom is simply a mass of thorns and wounds caused by it are slow to heal.

Our marshes, which are simply shallow lakes and ponds gradually filled in during the past ages by decaying vegetation in which cedar logs are still found at a great depth, when drained, make up some of our most valuable farming lands. These on the mountains are simply great beds of moss and down below it is almost like peat moss in character. While generally covered with water during the winter, they are nearly dry during the summer months.

It is in these marshes that the shrubs grow, the leaves of which were used by the early settlers as a substitute for tea. The leaves have a spicy, pungent flavor and are somewhat aromatic. They were known as Continental Tea. The marshes also have large quantities of the Sundew, the only carnivorous plant in these northern latitudes which tempt the unwary insect to its destruction with its glistening crystal bait.

The universal law of nature seems to be that nothing can live but by the destruction of some other life. Brute force seems to rule the world, even among men. Tis little wonder that Germany, harking back to middle age culture should have made "might makes right" her motto, even when the best of us either as individuals or nations, are so prone to be governed only by self interest.

Our organization of the Episcopal Church seemed to stimulate the few Methodists to do likewise so they held services in the schoolhouse for a while under a number of ministers. The ablest of whom was part Indian who lived on the old Sam Brown place. This preacher, a Mr. John Tennant, succeeded through a revival, in getting quite a number to join the Church.

Sometime after he left they prepared to build their church by holding a second Revival. This time they got William Wright and his wife, who, through fear of death and Hell, became their Angel. He loaned them the greater part of the money necessary. "Col." May needed whitewashing badly so he got converted and went around hugging old Allan Robinson, his lifetime enemy who had got scared into church by failing health and was really trying to hedge against the Devil.

But "Col." May was troubled with no such softening of the brain as the customs officers just then caught a large shipment of opium in his shipment of apples which was consigned to his pal in Seattle.

Among the men who had leased the Langdon Lime Works at various times was William Shipley, who became one of our very best friends. His family and ours visited together quite a good deal. Mrs. Shipley, who was a very nice lady, became your Mother's chum, for she, like myself, has always been slow in making friends.

As previously stated I was continually in hot water with Rev. Gray on account of his recklessness in church expenditures and his failure to report money received. He induced us of the vestry to go on a joint note for $500 for material for an addition to the church pledging us that he would get the amount long before it was due. When the time arrived and he had not made good, I took my part of it and asked the others to join me and pay it off, but Gray interfered and told them to just give him a new note in its place and he'd soon get it from his church friends. Also, while they were about it, they could make it for $750 as a little extra money would sure come in handy. This angered me and I told them that I stood ready to pay my share of the $500 but if they gave a new note I certainly would not go on it. Nor would I pay one cent on it when it came due. I handed in my resignation as treasurer. Hambly said, "Let him go, we can get along without him." But Gray said, "By no means. I'd rather have any other dozen men down on me than Tulloch". So I kept off the note and after Rev. Gray left the area they had it all to pay.

I remember one evening I went up to pay $5 I owed at the store and Dean Watson of Seattle was there holding services. I went into the church and when they took up the inevitable collection, I put in a nickel, I supposed, knowing that I had one in my pocket. Then I remembered about the $5 and found it was gone and the nickel was still there.

After services I mentioned it to Rev. Gray. He laughed and said he guessed the church was that much ahead. When he looked in the sack and found the $5 gold piece, he asked Dean Watson what he would do under the circumstances. The Dean told us of one of his members who had by mistake dropped a marked silver dollar in the collection plate which was a family heirloom. The man wanted to give another dollar in exchange, but the Dean told him that a $20 gold piece was about the same size and that they would settle on that basis, which they did.

I said "All right, Rev. Gray, you keep my $5 and I'll deduct it from your stipend." This didn't seem to please him. In fact, it seemed to take all the fun out of the joke.

Another time Gray came to me late at night to have me endorse a note for him for several hundred dollars, which I positively refused to do. He was very angry about it, but I never would endorse anyone's note and certainly not his, for he never paid anything.

Rev. Gray brought in a lot of so-called missionary goods from his church people in the east and proceeded to make himself solid by distributing them among his church members.

I indignantly refused them, telling him that I was not a pauper, that I paid for all my family wore. The whole thing was a fraud as the members of his church were not subjects of charity, but were all fairly well to do. I told him I wouldn't touch the stuff with a ten-foot pole. Gray said "That's just some of your Scotch pride again."

Though I had more to do with Gray than anyone else on the island, I never lost a cent by him and he left a great many checks with no funds to pay them when he left Orcas Island. With all of his misdoings, he was a man of so much personal magnetism and so much intelligence that it was impossible not to like him.

14.

The fruit grown on our island was of such superior quality that Orcas Island soon became widely known and Gray, taking advantage of this, induced a number of Seattle men, among whom were David Baxter, W.A. Peters, Ed Meany, J.D. Lowman and Dean Watson, to organize the Orcas Fruit Company. Through this organization they purchased the farms of Charles Setzer and Amos Hill and a tract that lay between and close to Hambly. Thomas Dixon, S.R.S. Gray and I acted as Board of Directors which gave us each a few shares of the stock and a salary of $4 per day while employed on company business.

I was the only one of the four who was a practical orchardist so the Seattle gentlemen soon gave me to understand that they were looking to me to prevent waste and extravagance. Things ran along fairly well for the first year and we got quite a tract in readiness for planting in apples, when Gray became enthused with the Italian Prune craze, which was sweeping the state. He put up a job with Van Gohren who had a stock of several thousand young prune trees in his nursery which he was anxious to unload. In spite of my protests he closed the deal with Van Gohren in my absence as the other members did pretty much as he told them. I sent in my resignation at once, but Baxter begged me to remain a little longer, which I did.

However, six months later I withdrew and Baxter paid me in full for my shares. The stockholders' money continued to be most shamefully squandered until their property had cost them about $85,000 and their assets were not worth more than $20,000 at the most. Had my advice been followed and only apples and pears of tried varieties been planted the company would certainly have made good.

I had noted the good results of my irrigation, not only on my small fruits and garden, but upon my fruit trees also. Although Puget Sound country has a name for being the wet one, owing to the number of showery days during the winter, it is in reality the very opposite. For its long summer months are practically rainless.

I believed that by irrigating I could make many kinds of my trees everbearing that were only bearing in alternate years. Being in Seattle shortly after the great fire and seeing tons of twisted pipe from the burned district being sold as junk, I thought that for irrigating my south orchard it would be fine. I could straighten out the pipe and make it carry water from the stream to a tank. So I went into partnership with E.E. King, who also wanted to try it. We each bore half the expenses.

I then went to Seattle and put in a very strenuous week digging the pipe out of the debris and partly straightening it so it could be loaded on the vessel. I got the Point Arena to bring it down for me and it was a hard looking lot of freight, sure enough. All sizes, all lengths and so crooked it would not lay still. I bought pipe cutters, dies and couplings for all the sizes and King and I had a man-sized job of getting the old junk into some kind of shape, as the fire had hardened the pipe so that it was almost impossible to cut threads in it. We finally had to make great wooden couplings and cork them with oakum.

We built a tank on the line between our two farms, which happened to be the highest ground. We also used the water on alternate days. After a few years I became dissatisfied with it as it only took the water from the foot of Mt. Constitution while I wanted to utilize some of the thousand feet of the fall from the spring above. Thus I could reach the whole of my farm and also supply water to my house and barn with enough pressure for a fountain. With this fine stream tumbling down the mountainside I had long dreamed of making our home beautiful.

90

I went to Seattle and bought half a mile of from one to one-and-a-half inches in size of pipe and laid it from the spring to the house, chaining it to the trees to keep it from sliding. We laid a branch toward the barn and put in a fountain at the foot of the garden which threw up a beautiful spray for thirty feet or more. After we had built our two fish ponds of 1-1/2 acres each and stocked them with Rainbow trout from Colorado, our place with its white shell road, its fish ponds, orchards and its fountain became the showplace of Orcas Island. It also became the favorite drive for tourists and the arch over the gate with Glenwood painted on it became well known throughout the country. I tried to get others to give their homes a name and beautify them, for aside from the pleasure they would derive from it, I knew that it would be a valuable asset. But only a few did it.

While we took pride in our home, our occupation of fruit growing involved ceaseless and increasing toil for us. Although in the early years it had been not only profitable but comparatively easy, but lately it had become the most slavish of all occupations. This was due to the many introductions of so many insects and fungus pests which made almost continuous spraying necessary. It was both extremely costly and laborious and the ever-increasing prices of boxes and freight and the extortion of the pirates of Western Avenue, was fast making fruit growing a losing business. But our place had cost us so much that we believed it better to hang on until we could get what we considered a reasonable price for it, rather than to sell it at a sacrifice.

About this time we had a call from a gentleman from Denver, Colorado named Charles Bancroft Walker, who became for the remaining years of his life our best friend and his name will be a household word with all of my children while life lasts. Mr. Walker was a cousin of Bancroft, the historian, and was himself an author of some note. Chief of his works being "*The Footprints of Time*" and the "*Mississippi Valley*". These works dealt largely into the research of the life and habits of the Mound Builders and their relation to the Aztecs of Mexico.

91

Charles Bancroft Walker had seen some of my correspondence with eastern papers as well as some mention of my work in a book describing the Islands of the Archipelago, written by a lady tourist some years ago. He came to see for himself if things were as good as reported. He was satisfied with the climate, soil and location and bought five acres from me at the foot of Mt. Constitution. Here he could not only get all the water he desired for irrigating of the terraces he planned constructing, but where the sun beating against the mountain in that sheltered location gave him an opportunity to experiment with subtropical fruits and nuts. (Editor's note: at this writing, 1977, these terraces can still be seen).

Here he spent his time gardening and writing the work he was then engaged in writing. During his spare time he taught our children in those branches our common school could not. But unfortunately the head of the publishing house in Denver, with which he dealt, sent an urgent request that he come back there for a time.

While there they took him on an outing to the summit of Pikes Peak and the change from our sea level to that of high altitude was too great for him at his age and brought on dysentery. He hurried back to us, but was only a shadow of his former self. That autumn, when my children were all sick with pleurisy which was then an epidemic, Mr. Walker was with us every day caring for them. I feared much that he also would take it (pleurisy) and when one day he failed to appear, I went to see him and found him shaking with the ague. I sent for the doctor at once, but when he came he jollied him up and told him he'd be all right in a few days. However, on his way home the doctor sent me word to prepare Mr. Walker for death, for he would not live but a day or so at the most.

That was the hardest task I ever had to perform. The old gentleman took it like the brave man he was. His only regret was that he could not finish the work he was writing. He lingered along a day or two, during which he once said to me, "Mr. Tulloch, your childrens' love has been the crowning glory of my old age." And the poor children could not even bid him

92

James Francis Tulloch and son, Stuart, fishing from their homemade wharf at the Tulloch home on Orcas Island sometime in the late 1800's. Stuart, the last living son of James and Annie Tulloch, passed away in June of 1976.

James Tulloch made his home on Orcas Island from 1875 until 1910. Shown here is the original Tulloch family. The picture was taken just outside their Orcas Island home. Back row: Ida, Glenn, Lorna, James Francis, Ross, Laura, Norman and Eva. Front row: Annie Brown Tulloch, Stuart and Isabel.

an eternal farewell or attend the funeral, for they were very low and delirious. Those were sad days indeed for all of us. Our children being young, survived, but our best friend was lost to us. And a sweeter nature in a human I have never known.

Charles Bancroft Walker had been for many years a minister of the Methodist Church, but careful investigation had satisfied him that those orthodox doctrines and beliefs were errors. So he kindly bade his brother ministers goodbye, wishing them well, but telling them plainly that he could not continue to preach that idea of God. He was convinced that it was a wrong one. When I wrote to his sister in New England announcing his death and got a reply, she said she hoped God would overlook his apostacy and not damn him eternally. Maybe you think I didn't tell her just what I thought of her and her unchristian and unsisterly letter.

15.

I have never been a good mixer as a certain reserve which I could not overcome seemed to keep others at a distance. But I certainly did enjoy the companionship of those I called my friends. And I have reason to be proud of them for they were men and women with whom anyone might be proud to associate with. Among them were Mr. and Mrs. Brooks, Will Donnecan, Wm. B. Warren, Rev. Sloan, J.H. Swerdfiger, R.R. Cockerall, Thomas Lee, H.W. Harding, Mrs. Emily Gow, Wm. Shipley, Charles B. Walker and the children's good little grandmother, Mrs. Eleanor Setzer.

I had a number of acquaintances that I liked of course, but these were my real friends. Of course I am not referring to my kinfolk, as my childrens' marriages have just added to our family group. The enduring friendship which lasted through life between Mrs. Setzer and I surely gave lie to that Mother-in-law business, for she was always as good as gold to me and her death was a great loss to us.

These islands from whose fruit growing qualities we had hoped for so much became quite overshadowed by the extensive volcanic districts of Eastern Washington, whose easily prepared and rich volcanic soils gave a much higher colored fruit. Though the flavor was not equal to our fruits, the attractiveness of the Eastern Washington fruit soon drove ours off the market.

The grain raising districts of San Juan and Lopez Islands were almost forgotten in the immense agricultural lands of Whatcom, Skagit, Snohomish and Pierce Counties which stretch their fertile valleys between the Cascades and Puget Sound. These lands yield almost fabulous crops of all the cereals. But the rocky islands forming this archipelago in the Sound and the Gulf of Georgia are destined to be the cradle of the race that will dominate this great Western Ocean in the future.

For just as the rocky shores of New England manned the Clipper ships of Continental days, our islands will be the source of the manpower of the great merchant machine which will make our flag known in all ports of the world. Now that we have reclaimed and possessed the continent our race will go ever westward and possess the ocean also. And what a place these islands are as a cradle for seamen. For the sea is their only highway and they dream of the ocean and its ships from their infancy. No better school can be found to make good neighbors than these waters, for it certainly requires a cool clear head and a steady hand to find one's way through these dangerous channels in the darkness, or what is even worse, the dense fog, yet accidents rarely occur.

The storms in the Straits and the Gulf are so fierce that the deep sea sailors dread them. Yet our little mail steamers seldom ever turn back or lay over, even when the big ocean liners have to seek a port.

This reminds me of a trip I made across the Straits in our little mail steamer when we ran into a fierce gale which made our boat do some queer acrobatics. An old deep sea captain and I were both hanging to the casing of a cabin window which gave us a hand hold and kept us from having our brains dashed out against the side of the vessel. One moment we'd be looking into the green sea and the next our feet would be flung from under us and we'd be staring at the sky. One minute the boat would be setting on her stern, the next diving toward the bottom with her propeller racing in the air. Never the same thing for two minutes at a time.

When I said in disgust, "I wish this darned old tub would make up her mind which side she likes best and stay there," the old Captain turned a face to me that was stamped with mortal fear and said, "Young man, she'll soon find the side she'll lay on and she'll lay there eternally." I told him to guess again for I had confidence in our captain and in our little boat.

When we got across we found that the big Alaska ships had had to turn back and seek shelter. These waters, owing to the many islands and the crooked channels make even old sailors subject to seasickness during such storms, for unlike the long regular waves of the ocean we never know from one moment to the next just what to expect.

Captain Beecher told me that on one of his trips down from Vancouver Island in the old Evangel when she struck a storm in the Gulf, during the storm he sent a sailor below to coil away a quantity of rope, which he did. But he came up looking like a dead man and upon arriving at Port Townsend, he quit. When Captain Beecher asked his reason for quitting, as he was a good man, he said, "Captain, I've been a deep sea sailor for forty years. I've been on every sea and in nearly every port on earth. I've shipped on windjammers and teakettles and most everything that floats and I never knew what it was to be seasick until I struck this damned inland pond. I can stand the water going two ways at once, but here it goes all ways at the same time and this gets my goat."

We finally got rid of old "Col." May who, finding his smuggling schemes too closely watched, sold his place and moved to Taos, Mexico, where he soon had gambled everything away as he met gamblers who were more than a match for him. When next heard of he was appealing to the Masonic Lodge in Port Townsend for help. He died in Taos shortly after in penury and so had passed a man who, low and coarse with a certain amount of ability and a very great energy but always used it for unworthy purposes.

It was generally believed that he and the gang of Indians he kept around him were responsible for some of the murders that occurred. Your Mother was terribly worried while I carried the mail over the lonely route to Doe Bay where, for a great part of the way I had to crawl through brush and where I could easily have been shot from the wayside and no one the wiser.

97

I recall of hearing of May telling Mr. Setzer of how I had balked some of his schemes and Mr. Setzer said, "Yes, but you must admit he's pretty smart." May replied, "I know he is, damn it, and I hate him."

Shortly after moving to our new house I got a fall that nearly used me up. Ross and I were returning from the west side of the island one cold night with some stock hogs in the wagon and the doubled box was on it. The spring seat was quite high up and Ross, having heavy gloves on, had poor command of the team which ran away circling the yard and upsetting the wagon throwing me out on the rocks behind the house. I landed on my head and breast and was severely hurt.

After I quit carrying the mail I got a cart from Seattle and tried to utilize the pony but it was no use. He was a cayuse and fit only for riding and even then one had always to be on guard or be thrown by its shying. Ed King once borrowed the pony and contrary to my advice put his mother-in-law, Mrs. Durkee, on him, with the result that he landed her in the road with a broken wrist. But King, who was rather conceited about his horsemanship, declared that he could break him to work if I would sell him cheap.

I sold King the pony for $15 and he started to break him. He made a kind of stone boat with shafts which he called a "go-devil" and took the pony out to a bare place among the trees in plain sight of the house. So naturally, we took in the circus. King and his two brothers covered the pony's eyes and hitched him to the contraption and upon removing the sack the pony gave one glance behind and the fun began.

The King boys each ran for a tree from behind which they peeped like Indians as the "go-devil" circled like a Catherine wheel. When the seance was over there was no "go-devil" left, but there was a pony with a broken leg which had to be shot. And singular to relate, King did not brag of his superior horsemanship for some time.

16.

I had for some years ceased to vote the Republican ticket, as the party had become very corrupt. While claiming to be the party of Lincoln, it was trying to undo his work and had become simply a tool of Wall Street and the Corporate interests. When we, who had suffered so often from Wall Street-made panics, saw a movement among the Independent voters toward organizing a new party whose object would be to restore power to the common people, we welcomed it.

Though I was never an extremist, or radical, I was aware that our Anglo Saxon people are naturally conservative and make political changes one step at a time. I recognized that Bryan's battle cry of "16 to 1" must appeal very strongly to the west and even if not successful it would tend to consolidate it and make it feel its strength. If successful it would not only greatly stimulate our silver mining industry, but so increase our circulating medium as to revive business over the whole country.

For the selfish people on Wall Street had so constructed the currency that their gold on which they had a corner, had an undue purchasing power. As to the other things advocated by the party I recognized that while good and just in themselves, it was hopeless to expect to win them now. But that was no reason they should not be advocated. Quite the contrary, for only by such political discussions can progress be made.

While I had little or no hope of the immediate success of the peoples' party, and could not be blind to the fact that like all new popular movements, it drew to it all the cranks and ill-balanced extremists as well as the self-seekers who could not

99

get their feet in the public trough through adherence to the old parties.

I became a member, though never what they called a middle of the road member. One great reason for my joining this political party was the wish that through it we might be able to break up the Republican ring that had so long misruled our country. A courthouse gang headed by John S. McMillan of Roche Harbor our elections were little more than a farce. All we had to show for our high taxes was a ring of high salaried officials who fed the people on their fine election promises which they never kept.

This McMillan was a lawyer from Tacoma who had become the superintendent of the Roche Harbor Lime Works and by pretending piety and crafty wirepulling, had made himself so much the political boss that he carried the vote of San Juan County in his vest pocket. Delegates from the Republican Conventions admitted to me that the typewritten list of candidates he carried in his vest pocket was chosen bodily without discussion. Tis little wonder he was nicknamed the Grand Duke for he certainly ruled the party with an iron hand. He had a consuming ambition to become a United States Senator and he counted on using our county as a stepping stone. I certainly felt like doing what I could towards blocking his game.

We had organized a Farmers Co-operative Association a year or so before which, in spite of its high sounding name, was chiefly intended as a public association where people of the various islands could meet together each summer and get acquainted and enjoy themselves. We thought that we could overcome to a great extent the insular jealousy that had prevented our working together for a common cause.

We had acquired a place for holding it on the south side of Shaw Island as that was the center of the group. Our meetings were both enjoyable and beneficial, being devoted to lectures, dancing, visiting and to the discussion of all subjects of public interest. This being campaign year the political pot was already beginning to boil. We of course expected to discuss political matters as well.

We had erected our arbor the year before but as we were late in arriving this year we expected that ours would be preempted as it was first come first served. But upon rounding the point in our boat we were met with a shout of welcome and found our arbor reserved for us with our name printed on it. This kindness pleased us very much.

After a few hours spent in renewing old acquaintances and making new ones the subject of politics came up. There were several office hungry parties present, chief among them was a Friday Harbor lawyer named Nordyke who was burning with anxiety to serve the dear people if they would only give him the nomination for State Senator. His greed for office disgusted me and I doubted his honesty but I saw he would get the nomination, as he had practically no opposition. Our people seemed to care only about who would be their representative.

That night we held a mass meeting and I got a very unpleasant surprise for as soon as the meeting was called to order, they sprang my name for the head of the ticket. I positively refused to run. I told them I would do my best for their candidate, whoever he was, but that I would not hold it. Your Mother joined me in this because aside from my dislike for office holding of any kind, though I had never been free from small ones such as road superintendent, school director, etc., I had agreed with her that I would never be a candidate for anything that would take me away from home. For we wanted peace and quiet and a chance to raise our family as they should be raised.

Such a storm you never saw. They came at us from all sides. One grabbed me from one side and said that I must consent as the Republicans would be with me, for they were sick of the party. Another declared that the Democrats had already chosen me as the one to break up the courthouse ring, and the people's party said it would be betraying the party if I refused to run. I tried to nominate a Lopez Island man who I knew wanted the nomination but they would not hear of it.

After a long fight in which I fought harder to escape the nomination than ever a man did to win one, they forced an unwilling consent from me and your Mother and I retired.

The crowd, having gained their point, kept up a jollification most of the night. The Democrats joined with us and the list of candidates was made up from the two organizations. They were sure of success in which I did not agree with them and cautioned them against over-confidence. For I knew San Juan County was overwhelmingly Republican. Although many made us all kinds of promises of support I knew that at the last they would be whipped into the traces as usual.

I put my private affairs in shape so that I could devote my time to the campaign and make a house to house canvas of the county. But I never deceived myself that we had anything but an uphill fight. During the whole campaign I never once asked a man to vote for me. My sole object was to wake up the farmers to the fact that they were being plundered and that party names mean nothing. The one great satisfaction I got out of the campaign was the opportunity it gave me to meet the people in their homes.

One amusing incident was when one of the Republican workers, mistaking me for Eb Harrison, whom I somewhat resembled, came to me and very secretly began to unfold a dirty trick he said would put us in bad with the voters. Before he had proceeded far I told him who I was and he was about the silliest person I ever saw. My party blamed me for not letting him give his scheme away.

The editors of our party paper asked me for a statement of our party's aims which was carried by the paper during the campaign. This seemed to annoy the Republicans and they replied with a screed by a fellow named Gould. Gould was from Seattle and came to the county with about $25,000. He set up a little note shaving institution which he called a bank. By loaning small sums to the needy farmers at usurious interest rates he soon became a considerable property holder. Recognizing the trend in county politics he became an enthusiastic Republican. In his rather abusive screed Gould closed by saying that the nomination had been forced on me and that my sole ambition was to stay on my farm and look after my horses and cows. For once he came pretty near the truth.

After we had canvassed the north end of San Juan Island I came back to Friday Harbor in company with Ed Delaney who was running for sheriff and a Mr. Rose of Shaw Island who was our candidate for treasurer. I was informed that my opponent, a young man named John L. Murray, who had been a school teacher in the county, had threatened to shoot me on sight for statements I was credited with having made. I went over to his office to see what the nonsense was all about. A crowd gathered in the street expecting to see some old campaign stuff. Murray met me very civilly and shook hands. We talked things over and when we came out and walked up the street together it seemed to be a real disappointment to them.

R.M. Gaines took me over to the south side of the island in his carriage and upon returning to Friday Harbor I met a large delegation of ours headed by J.L. Davis of Lopez Island, who was very angry and declared that the Democrats had betrayed us and headed by Ed Allen they were trying to set me aside to put a Democrat named Thomas in my place. After listening to their complaints I called a meeting of our party and the Democrats and sent a special request to Ed Allen, who came looking very much as though he had been caught stealing sheep.

Calling the meeting to order I stated what I had been told and reminded them I had been nominated but that I had not sought the nomination. I told them I was going to put it to a vote and that if half of them voted for Thomas I would resign at once, and that I would work harder for him than I ever had for myself. I said that if they could not make a decent showing for Thomas I would require a pledge from them that they would work faithfully for the ticket as it was.

I called on Allen, who pledged himself to do so and the vote stood all but two or three in favor of me. Allen left promising to do his best which he did as follows: He knew that his percentage of Waldron Island was almost solidly for us, so he took them away, including the election board, to Stuart Island

103

for herring fishing a day or two before election where on an excuse of rough weather, he kept them.

This dirty trick and the bringing in of the Republican barrel and the running free of every rum hole in the county, as well as other well known Republican election practices, carried the county by a vote of six if I remember correctly. But we threw such a scare into them that we broke up the old ring and badly shattered J.S. McMillan's little boomlet for Senator.

The story goes that a day before election my opponent felt so bad that he cried. This I do not believe, but he was terribly worried and I'm sure I do not begrudge him his success. He went to Olympia, voted with his party, drew his salary and came home while I returned no less pleased to my neglected work on the farm.

The next morning while I was hard at work in the field, Van Sant, my neighbor, a died-in-the-wool Republican, came over to jeer at me because we had lost. I thought it rather ungenerous of him as I had conducted a clean election campaign. So when he began to grin and said, "Well, how do you feel this morning?" I said, "I feel like Lazarus did." He asked "How's that?" I told him I felt like I'd been licked by dogs. For the first time Van Sant had nothing to say. The old gentleman went to Seattle to live shortly afterward and I had many a pleasant visit with him on my numerous business trips to that city. He had been a good neighbor and an honest man and his daughter, Belle, was one of your Mother's closest friends.

17.

At one of the meetings held by our Farmers' Association there was great indignation expressed at the high freight rates charged by the island steamers and I came in for a scoring because I got much better rates than the small shippers and because I always traveled on a pass. Because the others had to pay the high passenger fare charged, they demanded that as a personal friend of Captain Thomas I should try to get them equally low rates. I told them that I never asked for the pass but that it was given to me as I was the largest shipper on Orcas Island, except for the storekeepers, who also received passes. I recognized the justification of their compaint and had long hoped for the time when the farmers by sensible co-operation would overcome the handicap they were laboring under. I said I would do what I could and report to them at the next meeting.

I began my investigations by writing to the principal manufacturers of farm implements and machinery for their wholesale prices F.O.B. and to the Great Northern Railroad for its prices on carload lots laid down in Whatcom. Then to the main supply houses in San Francisco for ton rates on flour, sugar and other staples. I wrote to the shipping firms for their ton rates to Port Townsend. I then went to Seattle and arranged with several of the largest dealers in grain, hay and fruits to send an agent to bid on carload lots here on the islands (they required the Association to guarantee evenness in grade). This would overcome the farmers' greatest loss as he ships in small lots and must take whatever he is offered as he cannot afford to leave it there and pay high wharfage.

Having got things in shape, I went to Capt. Fred Thompson and asked him to give us ton rates to and from the cities by distributing as he went through by taking receipts from the wharfingers at various docks. On his return he would get his pay from the treasurer of the Association at the same tonnage rates given the stores. After hearing me through, Thompson said, "Your plan is a good one and if you were dealing with businessmen it would be a success, but these farmers will throw you down for sure."

But I finally got him to agree that if the farmers would bind themselves to ship only by his boat for a year he would give them the lesser rate. I called the people together on Shaw Island and laid my plans before them along with the Captain's conditions. I proved to them that aside from securing them against the sharks of Western Avenue in their shipments of produce, it would save them from 35 to 50 % in their purchases and make their farming a success.

Their reply was that they would see Capt. Thompson in hell first and they would ship by whom they damned pleased. So I bade them goodbye and handed in my resignation as a member of the Association. I thought I was through with it, but sometime after and during my illness, when I was fighting for life, I got a letter from Will Jenkins, Secretary of State, notifying me that the State tax for the Association had not been paid for two years and that my name had been given him by the Association as the one responsible for it. If the $12 was not paid at once he would levy on my property. I was one of the charter members. I had never been an officer of the Association and had resigned long before. While I realized the injustice, I was too sick to fight it, so I paid it and notified Jenkins that I was out of the Association for good.

I was very much disappointed with the course pursued by the farmers but that had been my experience with them through life. They will not pull together and they seem to be altogether lacking in business and political sense. With their membership and wealth, they might enact what laws they chose while in fact, they are simply the football of every slippery politician and they are plundered on every hand. They are flattered by the political spellbinders as the backbone of our government who send nothing but lawyers to look after their interests in our law making assemblies and in our markets they can neither fix the price of what they sell nor what they buy.

Among those whose friendship we especially enjoyed were Professor H.W. Harding and his sister, Mrs. Emily Gow. They spent a good many Saturday afternoons and Sundays with us, either fishing in our ponds and on our docks, or picnicking on the mountainside. We were always glad to meet them, but we never could like Mr. Gow as his whole life seemed to be devoted to money-getting. Although quite wealthy, he seemed to begrudge his wife every cent she spent. What a disease this money making greed becomes. But Mrs. Gow and Professor Harding were just the opposite and considered money of value only for the good it could do for others or the comforts it could purchase. They have both gone now, to the reward of a well spent life and we miss them greatly.

One year after Mr. Walker's death my health, which had been failing for some time, ended in a final breakdown. I had retired after an especially bad day and woke about midnight with the most terrible nausea. I got a fire started in the kitchen stove and lay down there and soon began to shake with the ague. They sent Glenn for the doctor who lived some eight miles away. He arrived the next morning by which time I was in a raging fever and felt as though I could not do a man's work. The old doctor examined me and hurried away, telling his friends at Eastsound that I'd be dead by morning. When Glenn went for more medicine the next day he was surprised and said, "Why, ain't he dead yet?" Seeing that I was putting up a strong fight the doctor stuck pretty close and with the splendid faithful nursing of your Mother and the vitality given me by my Scotch ancestry, I got back on my feet again in a couple of years.

But I will never forget those two terrible years, one day burning up and with my heart seeming to jump from one side of my breast to the other and the next day the chill-clamming, cold of death creeping up my arms and legs and him experimenting with one deadly drug then another until it seemed as though he had run the whole gamut of materia medica, turning me into a veritable drugstore. Finally I got around to taking some interest in my affairs, which your good Mother and the boys had carried on in the meantime.

One thing I have overlooked which occurred before my breakdown was the organization of our school district. We had to send the children 2-1/2 miles to school at Eastsound, so I got those living on our Eastsound portion of the district to sign a petition for a new district and bond it for the money to build a schoolhouse. Of course this meant a fight with the Eastsounders, but we beat them. Then came the question of where the schoolhouse should be located as the new district was long and narrow.

The meeting which was called to vote on the issue was held in January and as a blizzard had just struck us, making travel difficult for ladies, I sent my team to the north end and brought them, though they came to vote against us. We out-voted them and when Jorgensen passed me shortly afterward without speaking, I asked him why he did so. I said I had sent a team for his voters. He said, "Yes, but you out-voted us and I'll never forgive you for that." They made me chairman of the Board of Directors and I filled that thankless position for several years.

18.

I had seen for sometime that I could not make fruit growing with all its drawbacks pay. As my boys were grown I knew they must begin their own lives. I knew too, that I could never afford to hire the help necessary to manage the orchards and farm. So I began to think seriously about selling the place and moving to some Sound city.

While your Mother and I were seriously discussing this proposition Von Gohren with true Prussian instinct was always on the lookout for some underhanded work. To secure our stream and to avoid a long drawn out lawsuit I got Ross to file a homestead on part of the mountainside. I took up the balance as a stone and timber claim. Having patented these we were safe as our land reached from the sea to the top of the mountain.

Shortly after we had completed these transactions a Mr. Griffin Hunter, who had organized a lime company with some ledges far up the mountainside, and who had bought a strip of land along my north line from Van Sant for a right-of-way to the coast, tried to seize part of my land, claiming that the survey was not correct. But I soon proved him a trespasser. He then tried to make your Mother's friend, Belle Van Sant give up a five-acre tract she owned for almost nothing, because he saw that she needed the money. She came to me with her troubles and though I did not want it, I gave her what she thought it was worth and several years later I sold it for a good advance.

Robert Moran, the builder of the battleship Nebraska and former mayor of Seattle had long been an admirer of Orcas Island and its beautiful lakes and now got control of the property of the Cascade Lumber Company and proceeded to build a palatial mansion there. He changed its name to Rosario. Through his agents he bought out all the farmers on Cascade Lake and along the south side of Mt. Constitution. This did not please me at all as I had worked hard to get the white settlers in there. They had built roads, established a school and were proceeding to build a church. Now it was all to be thrown away and given back to the wilds again just to gratify the pride of one man.

When I found that his agent lawyer was preparing to grab all the farms around Mountain Lake for unpaid taxes, the times being very hard, it vexed me very much as these people were my friends. About this time the owner of the old Nichols place wrote me from New Jersey where he was at work, asking me to try to get something more than the amount of the taxes owing on his property from Moran as he did not want to lose everything. I got power of attorney from the owner and then wrote Moran asking him to make a bid on the place. He replied that he did not want it at all. I had been notified by the county auditor that Moran's lawyer was after the property and that it was to be sold the next day unless the approximate $80 in taxes were paid at once.

This made me so angry at Moran that I asked the officials by phone to hold the property until the last moment as I was sending the money by steamer. I then had my son run all the way to Eastsound to catch the boat for Friday Harbor. Having paid the delinquent taxes I wrote the owner and told him what I had done. I told him I would pay him $100 more for his claim, or I would give him a reasonable time to repay me the tax money. Or I would hold the place for sale for him and pay all the costs.

As Moran owned all the rest of the property so that no road could be built to it I did not see much chance of selling it if Moran would not buy it. The man took my $100 and gladly sent me the deed saying that he was $100 better off than he had expected to be. He wished me luck in my gamble with Moran.

I let the property lie for a year or so before I approached Moran again as I knew that by then he'd have everything else he wanted. I then sold the property to Robert Moran for $1142. If he had dealt fairly with me in the first place he could have had it for about $200.

It was about this time that I struck off a few hundred circulars describing the beauty and advantages of Glenwood, our property, and started systematically to dispose of it. We got a number of applicants, but most of them came with promises rather than with cash.

I got one trading offer from Whatcom, but I did not want to live in that sleepy old place. I got another from Ballard, but that suburb of Seattle had too many drawbacks. I then put the property in the hands of Charles Somers Company of Seattle, but as they gave no satisfaction after a few months trial, I put it with the Calhoun, Denny & Ewing Co. They had, upon examining my descriptive circular, considered the land of importance enough to send a man down at once to examine it.

The man soon brought a Mr. and Mrs. Woodhurst who were charmed with the place and really wanted to buy it. But they wanted me to take their house and seven 25-foot lots as $7000 of the purchase price. Your Mother and I went to Seattle to see the property and found a large, 8-room modern house on it which they claimed had cost $42,000 to build. But the lots, while cleared and with small fruit trees on them, were badly cut up by a deep gorge which ran diagonally across them. I objected to the price set on the house and lots and wanted to cut it to $6,000 but they would not listen to that and the deal seemed to be off. However, upon talking things over at the office we finally agreed on terms.

I was to take the property at their figure and they would pay me $6,000 in cash and $3,000 in one year. As I had tried in vain to get $9,000 for the place previously, I was well content. But I am afraid your Mother was not, for she had become so attached to that rocky old island home that she left it with many regrets.

We made arrangements for a quick transfer and I made a trip downtown to make some arrangements. On my return home I found Isabel seriously sick. (Isabel is the daughter for whom James Tulloch was writing this diary). Instead of calling our old

111

family doctor the boys had called a newly graduated stripling of whom I knew nothing. Isabel grew much worse and Dr. Reed said her only chance for life was to send for a surgeon and have an operation performed for an absess in her ears.

He recommended a particular Whatcom surgeon and advised that a skilled nurse be brought in. I sent for both, but the islands are difficult to approach in stormy weather and they were windbound on one of the other islands and did not reach us here on Orcas Island until a day later. They put Isabel under with an anesthetic and lanced her ears, but she grew worse. The doctor told me there was no hope so I was allowed to see her, he having forbid it before, and the little one reproached me with not having been to see her.

I tried to keep up her courage by telling her of our home in Seattle, though it's little I cared where we went then. She brightened up at once and said we must get ready and she'd hurry and get well. This made me almost hopeful for I knew what a desire to get well is to the sick and I knew that she had inherited good vitality. She began to mend rapidly and in a little more than a week we moved away from Orcas Island where you children were all born and spent your youth, and took up our home in the Rainier Beach district of Seattle overlooking Lake Washington.

By now our two boys and two girls, Ross, Glenn, Ida and Laura had married before we left the islands. Ross married Mabel Fogg, a New England girl, Glenn married Nora Stroud of Deer Harbor on our island, Ida married Pierre Barnes, a patent attorney from Seattle and Laura married his brother, Horace Barnes, also a patent attorney from the same city.

This went far toward reconciling your Mother to the change as she could so easily visit her daughters. This locality in which we had now established our home lay on the slope overlooking Lake Washington and had been logged off by the Taylor Mill Company a few years previously. It was platted and put on the market by C.H. Sturtevant as a Rainier Beach addition to Seattle.

May 21, 1934. I resume my diary on the saddest day of my life for news has just been brought that Isabel, the youngest of our family, has left us. She it was who induced me to begin this record and claimed it for her inheritance when I am gone. But she has left us. I will go to her but she cannot return to us. A dear daughter, a true wife and a devoted and loving Mother. She has left her children and us a memory of the sweetest and best of women.

We in our old age cannot be reconciled to the thought that she should be taken and we left. There is so much that seems cruel and unjust, for while the Divine Plan is wise and great beyond human comprehension, the individual seems to suffer unjustly. But we feel that this short life is but one step in the eternal climb upward toward the perfection that is God. Our little girl has gone before us and may await our coming, which must be soon now, at the latest.

AFTERWORD

It is interesting to note that according to Al Magnuson, Publisher and Editor of *"The Islands' Sounder"*, bi-monthly newspaper of the San Juan Islands, the *"James Francis Tulloch Diary"* which ran serially for a number of months in that publication drew more letters and telephone calls than any other feature story yet to appear in that paper.

Perhaps one of the major reasons for such response from islanders and off-islanders alike, lies in the fact that Tulloch writes in unvarnished words what he and other early settlers went through in order to live on these islands 100 years ago.

Written at the request of his youngest child, Isabel, so that she and others of the Tulloch family might have a personal record of their family's history at the turn of the century, James Tulloch pointed out at the start of his diary why he wrote it:

"If in describing frontier life I might speak plainly of it as I found it, I sincerely hope that what I write for my daughter's amusement will never be allowed to hurt the feelings of anyone."

Although James Tulloch has written candidly about certain of his friends and acquaintances, the relatives of those he has written about who are still living have never taken offense at what he has said. Nor should they. After all, if one of our forebears was hanged as a horse thief, this surely doesn't make us a horse thief. I feel certain that in the eyes of the Lord we will all be judged solely by the manner in which we have conducted our own lives here on this plain.

At this point I would like to extend my sincere "thanks" to Mrs. Jessie Tulloch, wife of Stuart Tulloch, the last of the

Left to right: Stuart Tulloch, last living offspring of James and Annie Tulloch, who passed away in June of 1976; Mrs. Jessie Tulloch, Mr. and Mrs. Robert McRae. This picture was taken in the home of Stuart and Jessie Tulloch in November of 1975.

Stuart S. Tulloch—last of the original nine Tulloch children, all born on Orcas Island—was 87 years of age when he passed away in 1976. Stuart is holding the deed of trust to the original Tulloch home on Orcas Island in the San Juans. The Friday Harbor *Journal* he holds contains an article written by his father, James Tulloch. The article is reprinted in this book.

original James Francis Tulloch family, for permitting the publication of this unique bit of history. For it was she who felt that after the many years this diary had literally been locked up, that this generation, as well as generations to come, should be afforded an opportunity to read and enjoy some of San Juan Islands' history as it was lived by one family over 100 years ago.

Gordon Keith

NOTE: Sometime before the completion of this manuscript this editor received word from Mrs. Jessie Tulloch that her husband, Stuart, had passed away on June 10, 1976. Jessie and Stuart Tulloch had been happily married for sixty years.

ADDENDUM

Twenty-four years after James Francis Tulloch moved from Orcas Island to live out his remaining years in the Seattle area, a touching tribute to the San Juan Islands, written by this unusual man, appeared in the *Friday Harbor Journal*. Dated June 10, 1934, the article which follows is proof positive of James Tulloch's insight into nature as well as his command of the English language.

THE SEA GIRT ISLES OF SAN JUAN
by James Tulloch, Sr.

The Thousand Isles of the St. Lawrence have by their wonderful beauty long been the summer playground of the East, but we in the great northwest have our San Juan Archipelago, a beauty far exceeding anything to be found elsewhere in America. These Islands deserve far more attention from the tourist than they have received, as nowhere in America can such

116

varied and interesting scenery be seen with so little effort. Lying as this archipelago does, surrounded by the cities of Puget Sound and British Columbia, and within a few hours run by steamer from any of them, it robs travel of all its hardships.

Among the islands is a scene of beauty which unfolds at every turning. From the summit of Mt. Constitution on Orcas Island, 2409 feet high and overlooking the whole region of Puget Sound and the Gulf of Georgia is an unparalleled view of mountain and valley, sea and land. The silver winding channels among them make up a view which can be seen nowhere else in America.

Vancouver Island and the Olympic ranges are on the west, with their cloud-piercing snowy peaks. The Straits of Juan de Fuca, through which passes the commerce of the Orient, and the magnificent Cascade range on the east extends along the horizon from British Columbia to where it would be lost in the distance were it not for that grand old Mt. Rainier which refuses to be ignored as she looms heavenward. The whole of the magnificent Puget Sound region seems to lie before your very feet. The fertile lands of Whatcom, Skagit and Island counties with their thriving cities seem but little more than a stone's throw away.

Almost directly below, on a craggy bench to the eastward lie the twin Crater Lakes, small in size but of great depth and clearly showing their crater formation. The lava around the mountain foot in many places shows its volcanic character.

Lying between it and the lower mountains to the southeast is Mountain Lake, one and one-half miles long and of unknown depth. This beautiful lake, lying 1,000 feet above sea level, is well stocked with Rainbow and Cutthroat trout. Lower down is Cascade Lake, three-fourths of a mile in length and offering the angler like sport, while mountainsides are alive with deer, which with pheasants and quail should make this a paradise for the sportsman.

The two largest islands of the archipelago contain numerous lime ledges from sea level to about 1000 feet above. In one instance the remnant of a former ledge forms the apex of a

117

pinnacle on the mountain top. The sole remnant of the ledge was left by the war of the elements during long past ages. These ledges are composed of almost pure carbonate of lime, formed from vast shale deposits in an earlier geological age when this region was sunk in the ocean depths.

They contain little or no fossils but the over-lying sandstone and especially the Sucia Islands to the north are very rich in them. Their cliffs are a great resort for those in search of fossil treasures. The tourist from the east will find here much that is new and interesting in bird, animal and plant life.

In the sea, the mammoth kelp, with its ribbon-like leaves, often fifty feet in length, undulating with the wave or tide, are anchored firmly to the rocks many fathoms below. The varied and beautiful forms of sea shells of all shapes and sizes, the sea eggs on the rocky bottom with their many-colored spines, the sea cucumbers rest like immense slugs on the sandy bottom. The wonderful Sea Anemone is a "veritable sea-flower", which expands its beautiful colored flower-like form when undisturbed but withdraws snail-like within itself when touched. The barnacles covering all the rocks seem but a dead mass of shells when the tide is out but upon its return they become a scene of the most wonderful activity as the occupant of each little shell strikes out with its hand-like structure gathering in the food the returning tide has brought to its door.

The many tentacled star-fish, the spider-like devil fish, immortalized by Victor Hugo, the tumbling porpoise, that seem like boys at play, the huge black fish and other whales give an occasional call to announce their arrival by spouting. The countless salmon by the millions throng these island waters on their annual migration to their spawning grounds at the headwaters of the streams flowing into Puget Sound and the Gulf of Georgia. These and many other forms of life found here make this a veritable land of enchantment.

Along the rocky shores are to be found the beautiful madrona trees with their smooth polished bark and dark evergreen leaves. The gnarled and twisted junipers, the famous yew trees, from which the ancient Britons made their bows, while the lordly

118

Douglas fir in the lower lands tower from 200 to 250 feet in height and attain a diameter of six to eight feet. The mountainsides are covered with cedar, hemlock, tamarack, spruce, oak, soft maple, alder and willow. On the summit of Mt. Constitution is found a grove of stately white pine with their mammoth seed cones nearly a foot in length. On the very summit a few specimens of the sub-tropical manzaniti struggles for existence, although it is here reduced to a creeping shrub.

The marshes of the mountain grow a small native cranberry and spice shrub known locally as "continental tea" which served the early pioneers in lieu of the Asiatic article which was not obtainable. On every hand is seen the carniverous plant with its sparkling crystal trap set for unwary insect life. From the sea shore to the mountain top, the trees, rocks and lychens, while on the lower alluvial lands the giant ferns form veritable Lilliputian forests of six to eight feet in height, and so dense that progress through them is very difficult. But they furnish a home and hiding place for the numerous deer and other game.

On top of the mountain and over a thousand feet above any local supply, a beautiful spring of ice-cold water boils out of the rock. This water can have no other source than in the distant Cascade range some 40 miles to the east. This artesian spring must therefore flow many miles beneath the sea and rise and break forth on Mt. Constitution, the highest mountain between two distant ranges.

There is a larger artesian spring lower down the mountain, which with others becomes quite a stream as it flows into Glenwood Harbor on Eastsound. These springs are of the purest water, but on the south side, nearer sea level, there are a number of Chalybeate springs that are highly mineralized and in great demand by those in search of health.

This region, owing to its northern latitude and mountainous character, combined with the warm Japan ocean current that bathes its shores seems to be the meeting place of the sub-Arctic and the sub-tropical floras of North America. It offers an excellent field for investigation and study by the botanist and for the lover of nature in her most beautiful forms, nothing could

119

be more delightful than cruising among these lovely San Juan Islands, camping on their snow white beaches, or drifting with the tide along rocky shores in the early morning when the blue water reflects the forest-clad mountain above.

These are pleasures that remain in memory for a lifetime and the state of Washington has wisely chosen this beautiful region as a public park for future generations to enjoy.

CHRONOLOGICAL OWNERSHIP OF
THE JAMES FRANCIS TULLOCH PROPERTY
FROM 1883-1977

A chronological list of succeeding owners of the James Francis Tulloch property is reprinted in part from a report addressed to George and Lar Vern Keys by the Department of Conservation at Olympia, Washington.

Names and dates of land ownerships

James Tulloch, Patent 811, May 5, 1883. Tide lands included.

Also Patent 59, Sept. 25, 1907, Ross Tulloch, son of James Tulloch, patented a part, Patent 27, Feb. 17, 1904.

James deeded a portion to a son, Glen Tulloch. However Rose and Glen joined with James in the deed selling the property and it has all belonged under one ownership since that time.

James and Nancy Tulloch, Ross and Mable Tulloch, Glen A. and Dora E. Tulloch to Carrie L. Woodhurst and John J. Woodhurst, her husband, May 12, 1908.

Carrie L. Woodhurst and John J. Woodhurst, her husband, to James C. Lockwood, Feb. 21, 1911.

James B.C. Lockwood and Mary A.C. Lockwood to L.D. Pike, July 10, 1914.

L.D. Pike and Ella Pike to L.G. Pike Aug. 16, 1919.

L.G. Pike and Irene I. Pike to Susan B. Armstrong June 19, 1923.

120

Susan B. Armstrong to D.H. Smith Dec. 9, 1929.

Sarah Jane Smith, widow of D.H. Smith to George L. Keys and Lar Vern I. Keys Feb. 27, 1936. Took possession on Dec. 25, 1935, although deed was not filed until Feb. 27, 1936. (Lar Vern Keys was one of the original founders of the University of Alaska).

George L. Keys and Lar Vern I. Keys sold all of the acreage and the two ponds EXCEPT the old house and the north 100 feet of waterfront to Snohomish County Investment Company on Aug. 24, 1966.

In August of 1970 William Wood and Justine Foss Wood (daughter of the Foss Launch & Tug Company owners) purchased the property (acreage only) from Snohomish County Investment Company.

In November of 1973 Mr. and Mrs. William Wood purchased the old house and the north 100 feet of waterfront from Mr. and Mrs. Keys.

This was a homesteader's house up to 1890. After 1890 there were two. There was at least one homesteader's house and domestic use (water) and some irrigation up to 1889, two residences after that date, two lakes built, irrigation, gardens and orchards and fields, power for property, as well as domestic use for two residences.

Stuart Tulloch, son of James Tulloch, states in a letter to the Department of Conservation, that the lower lake was built about 1896 and the upper one about 1898.

"We had one government lot on the water, approximately 1320 feet.

"I was born in an old log house in the lower orchard in 1888. The house where you (Keys) live was built in 1889.

"We originally took our boxed apples by rowboat to the boats that ran to Bellingham (then called Whatcom) and Seattle. These boats were anchored in our harbor. Later we built a dock in the harbor with a runway and track with a flatcar which ran on an old mine car chassis."

A letter from Mrs. Kathryne White gives the following information:

"Before the second house was built in 1889 there was a hydraulic ram down near the shore in the lower orchard which took water to a high tank near the house. This furnished water for domestic purposes and irrigation."

(Mrs. White is the daughter of Glen Tulloch and granddaughter of James Tulloch.)

In June of 1977 William Wood as Trustee for Phillip Wood and Gary Wood sold the total property including the house to Mr. and Mrs. James Youngren.

Index

123

Sherer, J.L. 27
Shipley, William 86, 95
Slaughter, 11
Sloan, Rev. 95
Smith, Captain 11, 38, 52
Smith, D.H. 120
Snohomish County Investment Company 120
Stevenson, Miss 13, 25
Stevens, James 17
Stevens, John L. 4, 28
Still, Walter 69
Stockade Bay 9
Stone, Henry 24
Stroud, Nora 112
Stuart Island 103
Sturtevant, C.H. 112
Sucia Island 37, 80, 117
Sutherland, George 50
Swerdfiger, John 37-38
Sweeney Bros., Jo and Steven 37-38

T
Tacoma, Washington 4, 40, 47, 58, 77, 100
Teaser (Mail Boat) 22, 26
Tennant, John 85
Thatcher Pass 63
Thomas, Capt. Fred 105
Thompson, Capt. Fred 105
Tiffany, Mr. 76
Tilton, Theodore 7
Tom, Old 11
Tulloch, Alec 3
Tulloch, Charlie 3
Tulloch, Eva 56
Tulloch, Glenn 56, 76, 81, 107, 112, 119
Tulloch, Hugh 3
Tulloch, Ida 56, 112
Tulloch, Isabel 3, 111-113
Tulloch, James Francis 22, 113-114, 119-120
Tulloch, James (Justice of the Peace) 69
Tulloch, Jessie *11*, 114

Tulloch, Laura 112
Tulloch, Ross 33, 56, 76, 81, 88, 109, 112, 119
Tulloch, Stuart *11*, 114, 120
Tulloch, Will 3
Turtleback Mountain 49, 75-76, 81

V
Vancouver Island 74, 116
Van Sant, Mr. 49, 104, 109
Victoria, British Columbia 5, 10, 14, 16, 38, 40, 58, 60
Viereck 34-35
Von Gohren 89, 109

W
Waldron Island 34, 69, 103
Walker, Charles Bancroft 91-92, 94-95, 107
Warbass, Edward 15
Ward, John 2-3
Wardell, Wallace 24
Warren, William B. (Charlie) 37, 95
Waterman and Katy 60
Watson, Dean 43, 87, 89
Weeks, Mrs. 28
Welsh, Mr. 75
Whatcom 11, 36, 40, 46-47, 52, 58, 80, 95, 105, 111-112, 116, 120
Whidbey Island 63
White Beach 25
White, Katheryne 120
Whitner, Wesley 15
Winn, Judge 72
Wood, William 120
Woodhurst, Mr. & Mrs. John J. 111, 119, 120
Wright, William 11, 13-14, 20-21, 26, 33, 86

Y
Yesler 5
Youngren, James 120
Yott's Landing 28

Z
Ziegler, Mrs. 33-34